MODERN WORLD NATIONS

France

South Huntington Pub. Lib.
145 Pidgeon Hill Rd.
Huntington Sta., N.Y. 11746

Stephen C. Jett

Series Consulting Editor
Charles F. Gritzner
South Dakota State University

CHELSEA HOUSE
P U B L I S H E R S
A Haights Cross Communications Company

Philadelphia

Dedicated to the memory of
Jacques Robelin, Joséphine Clément, and Henriette Moureau,
and to Marie-Madeleine Robelin

Frontispiece: Flag of France

Cover: Paris with the Eiffel Tower in the distance.

CHELSEA HOUSE PUBLISHERS

VP, NEW PRODUCT DEVELOPMENT Sally Cheney
DIRECTOR OF PRODUCTION Kim Shinners
CREATIVE MANAGER Takeshi Takahashi
MANUFACTURING MANAGER Diann Grasse

Staff for FRANCE

EXECUTIVE EDITOR Lee Marcott
PRODUCTION ASSISTANT Megan Emery
PICTURE RESEARCHER 21st Century Publishing and Communications, Inc.
SERIES DESIGNER Takeshi Takahashi
COVER DESIGNER Keith Trego
LAYOUT 21st Century Publishing and Communications, Inc.

A Haights Cross Communications Company

http://www.chelseahouse.com

First Printing

1 3 5 7 9 8 6 4 2

Library of Congress Cataloging-in-Publication Data

Jett, Stephen C., 1938-
  France / by Stephen C. Jett and Lisa Roberts.
    p. cm. -- (Modern world nations)
Summary: Describes the history, geography, government, economy, people, and culture of
France. Includes bibliographical references and index.
  ISBN 0-7910-7607-5
  1. France--Juvenile literature. [1. France.] I. Roberts, Lisa. II. Title. III. Series.
  DC17.J48 2003
  944--dc22
                                                              2003013666

Table of Contents

France

The quiet French countryside gives no hint of the economic and political might wielded by this very modern and progressive country.

1

Introducing France

Old France, weighed down with history, prostrated by wars and
revolution, endlessly vacillating from greatness to decline, but
revived, century after century, by the genius of renewal.
CHARLES DE GAULLE

Historically and culturally, France is one of the most significant nations of Western Europe. The country is favored by nature, with a variety of landforms, climates, and resources as well as with rich and varied agricultural lands. Strategically, it is located between the Mediterranean Sea and the Atlantic Ocean. The country has played a pivotal economic, political, and cultural role in the history of its continent and of the world. It has particularly close historical and philosophical ties with the United States.

France is a roughly hexagonal country that bridges the gap between northwestern, mainly Germanic, Europe and southwestern, mostly Latin, Europe. In many ways it blends the best of both of those worlds. The beautiful French language is a descendant of the Latin of the Roman Empire. The name "France," however, reflects a Germanic legacy. It is derived from the Franks, a collection of early German tribes. King Clovis, the founder of France in 507 A.D., was a Frank. Likewise, Charlemagne, who, around 800 A.D. briefly unified what was to comprise modern France centuries later, was also a Frank. The logical, scientific, and military side of French character may reflect the Germanic legacy. On the other hand, the artistic, intuitive, and dramatic aspects of that character seem more a part of Mediterranean culture, especially that of Italy.

The French look to the Gauls—Celtic-speaking peoples related to the Scots, Irish, and Welsh, and whom the Romans conquered—as their ancestors. However, outside of Brittany, there is very little in the way of a detectable Celtic heritage in today's French culture.

The climate of northern France is similar to that of Britain and Germany, whereas the climate of much of the south is more like that of Italy and Spain. This climatic variety, coupled with its variety of landforms, allows France to produce a variety of agricultural products. This, in turn, contributes to a higher degree of self-sufficiency than possessed by most nations, and also to the fine and diverse cuisine for which France is so deservedly famous.

France faces two seas: the Mediterranean on the southeast and the Atlantic Ocean's Bay of Biscay and English Channel on the west. The country has 2,930 miles (4,716 kilometers) of coast. Not surprisingly,

France's geography—its pivotal location on the European continent and its lengthy coastlines—has greatly affected both its history and industries.

France has a long legacy of fishing for the "fruits of the sea" and of engaging in international maritime trade. Its naval and merchant fleets were key to the establishment of a once-vast overseas empire. In modern times, the coasts have offered many recreational opportunities. Today, the French excel at recreational and competitive sailing. Many French, as well as hordes of tourists from elsewhere, vacation along the Atlantic and Mediterranean shores, including the famous sunny Riviera. Vacation homes are popular in these and other attractive areas of *la belle France.*

France has important mountain chains. The lofty Alps extend deep into eastern France from neighboring Switzerland and Italy. The range includes glacier-flanked Mont Blanc, at 15,771 feet (4,807 meters) the highest point in Europe outside the Caucasus Mountains. France shares the Pyrenees with Spain; in fact, the crest of this range defines the boundary between these countries. The mountains are important sources of timber, support a large livestock industry, and provide spectacular scenery and skiing opportunities. Even more important, runoff from the mountains is the main source of water feeding the great rivers of Western Europe—the Rhine, Rhône, and Garonne—which are so important to transportation and agriculture.

For a nation of modest size and population, France has played a very important role in history. The country's influences in culture have been worldwide: art and architecture, music, theater and film, high fashion (*haute coûture*) and perfumes, and the culinary arts. One need only name such people as Claude Monet, Auguste Rodin, Claude Debussy, Molière, and Coco Chanel to recognize some of these contributions. Gothic architecture first emerged in the region near Paris, becoming the copied style of church buildings and universities worldwide. It was in the same region, centuries later, that French Impressionist painting was unveiled to the world.

For centuries, until surpassed by English, French was *the* language of diplomacy and general elite culture. Because of the Norman (French) conquest of England in 1066, English is particularly rich with French words. Perhaps 20% of the common English vocabulary comes from French.

Like Great Britain, and following the earlier examples of Spain and Portugal, during the eighteenth and nineteenth centuries France built an enormous empire that encircled the globe. Huge areas of Africa, especially in the northern half, became French colonies, as did substantial areas in Southeast Asia (French Indochina), and many Pacific Islands. The French also claimed parts of the Americas. France's possessions included French Canada, Louisiana (Territory), French Guiana, and various Caribbean islands. France exported French language, culture, technology, and institutions to these areas. Although most of the empire was dismantled following World War II, these former colonial possessions continue to reflect the French cultural legacy. They often retain French as an official language and, in many cases, still maintain fairly close political, economic, and cultural ties to France. French is the official or mother language of some 300 million people worldwide.

Owing in large part to this empire, France became an international economic force as well. This economic prominence has diminished in the postcolonial period, but is still very important. The empire provided plantation-produced tropical and subtropical agricultural products such as sugar, cacao (chocolate), tea, rice, coconuts, and dyestuffs, as well as mineral wealth. The colonies also represented a captive market for such French manufactured goods as textiles, tools and utensils, and machinery. In the colonies, ports, railroads, and highways were built. So were schools, hospitals, and other social-service facilities. Today, individuals of French descent are still significant in the bureaucracies and economies of many ex-colonies.

A French company constructed (1869) and co-controlled Egypt's Suez Canal that links the Mediterranean and Red seas. Because of this connection with Egypt, as well as its former colonial control over much of North Africa and parts of the Near East, France has a long-standing tie with the Arab world. The country also depends on that world for much of its petroleum, having very little oil of its own.

Although it also imports many goods, France is Western Europe's largest food-producer and exporter. Products include staple foodstuffs as well as specialty products such as gourmet cheeses, bottled waters like Perrier and Vichy and, above all, fine wine—which is, along with fashion, probably France's most famous product.

France has a long tradition of friendly association with the United States. French ships and troops were key to the success of the American Revolution for independence from Great Britain (France's traditional rival on the global scene). Much of American democratic philosophy is based on the writings of eighteenth-century French thinkers such as the Baron de Montesquieu, which caught the attention of Thomas Jefferson and other patriots. The United States came to the aid of Britain and France in World War I and World War II. Without American intervention, France could conceivably still be under German control today. The Statue of Liberty, which rises above New York Harbor as one of America's most familiar icons, was a gift from France to the United States in 1884.

France today is part of the European Union, which, thankfully, has replaced the old belligerent relations among such nation states as France, Britain, and Germany. With its rich history, countless cultural contributions to the global community, and contemporary importance in the emerging European Union, France is and will continue to be one of the world's foremost countries.

The French Alps near Chamonix represent only one of the many, varied landscapes that can be seen in a country smaller than the U.S. state of Texas.

2

Natural Environments and Landscapes

The land is varied and wealthy.
JOHN C. CAIRNS

France possesses a varied and productive physical environment. In this chapter, you will learn about the country's diverse land features, climates, soils, wild vegetation, and mineral resources.

LANDFORMS

Although considered a lowland country, France's physical geography is, in fact, extremely varied, ranging from high, rugged mountains to low-lying sandy coastal plains. Running northward and eastward through France is a major drainage divide. It runs roughly from the eastern Pyrenees, along the eastern highlands of the Massif Central and the crest of the Vosges Mountains in the northeast. To the north and west of the divide, rivers, including the Seine, Loire, and Garonne, run into the Atlantic Ocean. To the south and east, the rivers—most notably the Rhone— is the major stream draining into the Mediterranean Sea.

Geologic Forces and Landform Building

The mostly gentle and mature landscapes to the west of the drainage divide include the geologically old highlands of the Massif Central and the plateau of the Armorican Peninsula (Brittany), plus the Paris Basin and the Atlantic lowlands of the Aquitaine and Nantes basins. The Massif Central, Armorica, the Vosges, and the Ardennes (on the Belgian border) represent the eroded roots of very ancient mountain ranges. The sea encroached on these mountain roots and deposited thick sediments on and between them. Later still, gentle upward and downward bending, plus faulting, yielded the present highlands and the sedimentary basins adjacent to them.

The Massif Central (central highland), whose core corre-sponds approximately to the province of Auvergne and part of Limousin, is a high plateau. Parts of the Massif are quite rugged, the result of rivers cutting deeply into the uplands, exposing ancient rocks—and providing sites for modern hydroelectric installations. Later volcanic activity contributed lava flows, magma domes, now-extinct large volcanoes and smaller cinder cones (often with lakes in their craters), and rugged volcanic necks that appear as impressive isolated hills with steep sides. Many popular spas take advantage of the region's hot springs that are of volcanic origin. Dry limestone plateaus are found in the southern Massif and on its south-eastern and southwestern flanks. The roughness of a great deal of the Massif, plus the restricted quantity of good farm-land, has made much of the region one of relative isolation and limited prosperity. Livestock raising and cheese-making are important.

The Armorican upland of Brittany and parts of Normandy, separated from the Massif by the lower-elevation Poitou Gate, is of lesser size, elevation, and ruggedness. Much of it consists of rolling hills, although parts, in the Breton west, are higher, treeless heaths. The drowned coastlines are rugged, usually rocky and indented by bays and occasionally backed by cliffs. Small islands, including the mariner's landmark of Ushant (*Ile d'Ouessant*) off the tip, lie scattered around the peninsula. This interesting coast makes Brittany a favorite location for sailing enthusiasts and, of course, is important to commercial fishing.

Dividing the northeastern province of Alsace from adjacent Lorraine to the west, are the low, rounded Vosges Mountains, which contain ancient crystalline rocks. This wooded highland is bounded on the east by a major fault line, or break in Earth's crust along which movement has occurred, and it slopes off more gently toward the west.

Sedimentary basins form the great agricultural areas of France. In the north, the Paris Basin, drained by the Seine and Loire rivers, predominates. There, layers of marine limestone, chalk, and clays have formed a broad, shallow, roughly circular structural depression centering more or less on the capital and extending from the Seine headwaters to the English Channel. Erosion later exposed the various layers of rock, and the more resistant strata, especially in the basin's eastern half, form a series of limestone ridges. These ridges slope gently toward the basin's center. Many of the outward-facing scarps (steep faces) of these remain wooded, but in between are broad plains supporting some of France's richest farmlands.

In the southwest, the sedimentary Aquitaine Basin is also the basin of the Garonne River. The ever-broadening basin slopes northwestward from the Carcassone Gap between the Massif Central and the Pyrenees Mountains, down to the great Gironde estuary. Here, the Garonne and the Dordogne rivers meet near the important port city of Bordeaux and flow on to the Atlantic Ocean. The plains and low hills of parts of the region are planted with the grapes that produce the famous Bordeaux wines.

Alpine-Pyrenean France

The Vosges and the Massif Central are bordered on the east by two valleys created by fault lines. The Rhine River, which has its origin in the Swiss Alps, flows northward down the more northerly edge of these valleys. The other fault-created valley is that of the Rhône River, which flows out of Lake Geneva and then southward along with the Rhône's principal northern tributary, the Saône River. These two fault line-created valleys, of the Rhine and the Rhône, connected by the Burgundian Gate (Belfort Gap), form an ancient corridor for transportation and invasion. They are part of Alpine-Pyrenean France, named for the two truly high and rugged mountain ranges that lie partly within the country: the Pyrenees in the south are shared with Spain; the Alps, in the east, continue far eastward into Switzerland, Italy, Germany, and Austria.

These wrinkled and eroded ranges present some of France's finest scenery. Both ranges are relatively young. Some Pyrenean scenery is highly dramatic: there are many abrupt scarps caused by movements along the numerous fault lines. The Pyrenees, however, were not as extensively covered with glaciers during the Ice Age as were the Alps. As a result, their features are not as jagged. Hot springs occurring in the Pyrenees are the basis for several health-spa resorts. Hydroelectric facilities also have been built along a number of the rivers cascading from the range, and the power supports local manufacturing. Over thousands of years, these rivers have created an enormous stream-deposited plain along the mountain front that now supports productive agriculture.

The towering and heavily glaciated French Alps offer the country's most spectacular terrain. Alpine country attracts hundreds of thousands of tourists, hikers, skiers, and summer-home dwellers. As in the Pyrenees, many deep Alpine valleys

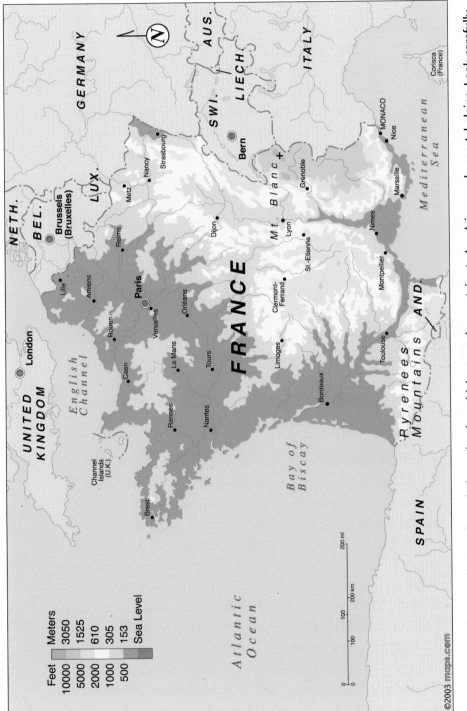

France's physical geography is quite varied, ranging from high, rugged mountains to low-lying sandy coastal plains. Look carefully at this close-up map of Western Europe to find rivers that begin in one country and end in another.

Feet | Meters
10000 | 3050
5000 | 1525
2000 | 610
1000 | 305
500 | 153
| Sea Level

©2003 maps.com

have been dammed and hold reservoirs used to generate hydroelectricity.

The Maritime Alps come right down to the Mediterranean and, in winter, snowy peaks back the resort towns of the Riviera. Despite the latter's fame as a seaside paradise, the steep, rocky coastline there produces small beaches covered with small, rounded stones rather than sand. The streams that descend steeply from the mountainous interior have cut deep limestone-walled gorges in some areas, of which the Grand Canyon of the Verdon is the best known.

Along Switzerland's northwestern border with France, separated from the Alps by the Swiss Plain flanking Bern, lies the Jura, a plateau and flanking ridges reminiscent of America's Appalachian Mountains. Because limestone is soluble under certain conditions, the Jura—like a number of areas in France—is riddled with caves, and much of the surface runoff disappears down sinkholes and into underground caverns. Nevertheless, the region boasts several rivers plus numerous lakes of glacial origin, and also has hydroelectric reservoirs. The Jura lent its name to the geological period known as the Jurassic (as in *Jurassic Park*).

Delta and Coastal Plain

Much of France's coastline is rocky and cliffed, but there are major exceptions. One such area is the delta at the mouth of the Rhône, where the river meets the Mediterranean and drops its load of sediment. This deposition has created a low, soggy landscape of mudflats and low-lying marshlands laced with stream channels, manmade canals, and landlocked lagoons. The delta, called the Camargue, is famous both for its bird life—notably, its huge flocks of pink flamingos—and for its raising of white horses and fighting bulls and their attendant "cowboys." Most of the delta area is protected as a national park or national reserve land. To the east of the Rhône delta is the large lagoon called l'Étang de Berre. Here, great oil refineries

A practical society, the French retain the most useful of traditional methods, such as this canal that transports goods, yet embrace new technologies like the super-fast TGV trains.

convert tanker-imported petroleum into gasoline and diesel fuel. There are long stretches of beach and lagoon country to the west of the Rhône as well.

A similar coastal landscape extends for some 125 miles (200 kilometers) along the Bay of Biscay from Bayonne in the south to the Gironde estuary in the north. This line of sandbar beaches forms a broad, low-lying, sandy coastal plain, the Landes, that is backed by lagoons and marshes. Patches of marshland occur to the north of the Gironde as well, notably on the coast of Poitou near the port city of La Rochelle. Some similar landscapes also appear on the coast of Picardy, in France's north.

SOILS

Soils are formed from disintegrated rock material by the combined influences of climate, vegetation, and slope—all working through thousands of years of time. In France, most soils developed beneath forest cover under conditions of temperate humid climates with relatively mild winters. Fortunately for France, these brown forest soils generally are excellent for agriculture. Soils formed on limestone (as in much of north-central and southeastern France) are particularly productive, because they are rich in nutrients and are light and easily worked. Many soils formed from volcanic materials (as those of Auvergne) are also fertile. Soils formed on sandy substrates, as in the Landes, are easily worked but low in nutrients, and are more suitable to growing coniferous trees than field crops. Mountain soils are generally thin and poor. Such soils commonly support livestock grazing and forests, rather than crop production.

WEATHER AND CLIMATE

France is blessed with relatively mild, midlatitude climates. Conditions can conveniently be divided into three main climatic zones: Atlantic France, Mediterranean France, and highland France.

On the Mediterranean coastline near Antibes, France, a seawall protects the homes nearby from the sea's destructive force.

Atlantic France: Marine West-Coast Climate

Although lying at latitudes comparable to Canada's New-foundland, northern France enjoys a temperate climate. West of the previously mentioned drainage divide, the country falls within what geographers call a marine west-coast climate. Here, weather is conditioned by prevailing westerly winds that blow in from the Atlantic across the relatively warm waters of the North Atlantic Drift, a continuation of the tropical Gulf

Stream that flows out of the Gulf of Mexico. Winds pick up moisture evaporated from the warm water and then precipitate that moisture onto the land, mainly in the form of rain.

Much of the moisture comes with cyclonic storms. Thus, gray, cloudy days are numerous throughout the year, especially in winter, and rain is common, though seldom intense or abundant. Autumn is the wettest season in most areas, with rain gradually diminishing into winter. Summer weather is often quite changeable, with clouds, rain, and sun following each other in rather rapid sequence; whatever the weather is doing at the moment, one can be sure that it will soon be doing something else. The farther inland one goes, and thus the farther from the oceanic source of moisture, the drier the air is and the more sunny days there are—although, of course, topography influences the local details of weather and climate.

Because the winds originate over the ocean, and since water moderates temperature extremes, climate in these parts of France is relatively mild, especially along the coasts. Summers are not especially hot, and winters not severely cold. Snow is uncommon, and when it falls it usually melts rapidly, except at higher elevations. Since there are no major land barriers to the inland penetration of the westerly winds until the Alps are reached, the marine west-coast climate extends far into the interior. As distance from the Atlantic increases, however, temperatures become less moderate. The mildest of all of the climates influenced by the Atlantic Ocean is in southwestern France, where the character of the dry-summer climate approaches that of the Mediterranean region.

Mediterranean France: Mediterranean Climate

What many people suggest is the world's most pleasant climate, the Mediterranean, extends along and behind France's Mediterranean Coast. Generally, it occurs in the area south of the Massif Central and the Alps, and extends northward up the Rhône Valley as far as Valence.

The Mediterranean coastline near Nice, France, experiences a climate that is ideal for tourism.

The typical Mediterranean climate is characterized by a dry-summer and wet-winter pattern. In parts of France, however, this pattern does not always occur because of mountain influences. Coastal areas experience very dry summers with rainy autumns and somewhat less rainy winters. Farther inland, autumn is the rainiest time as well, but spring also is quite wet and winter is somewhat drier. Summer can experience some rain, although normally not a great deal. In the lower-elevation areas, almost all precipitation falls in the form of rain. In the mountains, however, winter snowfall is common.

In winter, high atmospheric pressure lies over much of the region, keeping out maritime air and resulting in relatively dry conditions. This cold, dense, high-pressure air has a tendency to flow outward from the highlands and down into the valleys. In particular, it spills down the trench of the Rhône Valley in the form of an often strong, cold regional north wind called the *mistral*. Occasionally, mistrals even occur during summer months.

Highland France: Varied Mountain Climates

Highlands, particularly those facing moisture-carrying prevailing winds, catch moisture since they force winds to rise, cool, and precipitate their moisture loads. So, the mountains (especially, the upwind sides) are much better watered than are the lowlands, especially than those low areas in the south that are cut off from most Atlantic-origin moisture by the country's central uplands belt. Generally, the higher the elevation, the cooler the climate—which, along with greater precipitation, explains why, during the wintertime, snow accumulates in the Pyrenees, the Alps, and the Massif Central and, to a lesser extent, in France's other highlands. The spring-into-summer melting of this snow is the principal source of water in many of the country's river systems. The waters of these rivers permit not only boat and barge traffic, but also summertime irrigation of large areas in Provence, Gascony, and elsewhere.

WILD VEGETATION

"Wild vegetation" includes both natural, undisturbed vegetation, and spontaneously growing vegetation that reflects human modification of the environment. The distinction between fully natural and merely wild is particularly important in a country like France. Here, humans and their domesticated animals have been altering the land and its plant life for thousands of years. This alteration has included timbering, grazing, draining, agricultural clearing, plowing, burning, and planting, among other actions. Too, migrating humans and their animals have, for millennia, brought in new plant species, including both domesticates and weeds. Before human impacts became profound, most of France was forested, although parts of the south were covered with dense strands of shrubs (*maquis*). Today, only 27% of the land is wooded, much of which is in the form of deliberately planted tree "plantations."

ANIMAL LIFE

France's fauna, like its vegetation, is similar to that of the eastern United States. There are moles, bats, rats and mice, squirrels, rabbits and hares, deer, weasels, bears, and foxes. Unlike the United States, France also has hedgehogs and wild boars, and there are chamois (high-elevation antelope) in the Pyrenees and the Alps. Wild goats called ibex once roamed the Alpine highlands, but they have become extinct in France. Bird life of the United States and France also have a lot in common, but less so than among the mammals. Fish life is also similar. Other than vipers, poisonous reptiles are absent. Hunting is popular in rural France.

MINERAL RESOURCES

France has an abundant supply of many important mineral substances, among them quarried materials and mineral waters. A number of other mineral materials, including ores and fossil fuels, are available in small quantities, but the country must rely on imports to meet the demands of its large population and hungry industries.

Quarried Materials and Ores

All modern countries use large quantities of quarried materials for constructing buildings, highways, and other structures. France has ample building resources. Each year, quarries yield hundreds of tons of construction stone. They also produce dolomite for cement making, gravel and sand for mixing concrete and making glass, and clay for brick, tile, and pottery manufacture. Quarried limestone is used as flux in iron smelting. Most of these materials are very widespread.

France is less well endowed with metallic ores. Iron deposits, which have had great strategic significance in modern times, are concentrated in Lorraine, where ore masses are very large, though of relatively low quality. Foreign ore must now be imported. Additional reserves occur in Brittany and Normandy, and there is some iron in the Pyrenees as well. France is a leading iron producer, and iron and steel, in turn, are the foundation of many manufacturing industries in the north. Large bauxite deposits once placed France among the world's top producers of aluminum as well. However, cheaper overseas ores and declining demand have caused French bauxite mining to cease. The country also mines small quantities of tin, lead, zinc, and tungsten in Brittany and the Massif Central. Most other metals must be largely or entirely imported. Potash, mined for fertilizers, is an important product of Alsace and salt is also mined.

Fossil Fuels and Uranium

Among the energy resources required to operate a modern industrial economy, France is most favored in coal—the fossil fuel that heats homes (although much less today than formerly), smelts ores, and runs electrical power plants, not to mention its role as a raw material for manufacture of synthetics. But France's coal deposits are hard to extract, domestic labor costs are high, and the types of coal domestically available do not correspond well to industry's requirements. Therefore, France imports large amounts of anthracite and coking coals from a number of countries around the world.

France lacks adequate petroleum resources, a major weakness in the country's energy economy. Small quantities of oil have been found and extracted, but the country produces only about 3% of its demand for oil. As a result, France is obliged to import petroleum, most of which comes from Saudi Arabia and other Middle Eastern countries, Nigeria, and the North Sea fields held by the United Kingdom and Norway. This is one reason the country attempts to keep on good terms with the Arab world.

Elf-Aquitaine is a major French producer of gasoline and diesel fuel. There is a high tax on gasoline, intended as a disincentive to consumption. Although this has encouraged fuel-efficient cars, it has not discouraged the French from driving. The country also depends heavily upon natural gas, most of which is imported from Algeria, Norway's North Sea fields, and the former Soviet Union.

Following the petroleum crisis of 1973–1974, France decided that its electrical-energy future lay largely in nuclear power. Uranium, the source of that power, is fairly abundant in the country. Nearly 60 nuclear power plants are now in operation, supplying over three-quarters of the country's electrical energy (compared to 20% in the United States) and making France the globe's most nuclear-dependent country. These plants require large amounts of water, and are concentrated along the Rhône, Loire, and Garonne rivers, and on the English Channel coast. State-owned Éléctricité de France (ÉDF) is the world's largest power producer.

Contemporary energy conservation efforts have led to substantial savings of both electrical power and petroleum. Little progress has been made, however, in developing such renewable energy sources as solar-generated power. As a result, France still imports over half of its energy.

Mineral Waters

Perhaps only France, among the world's countries, would include mineral water among its important mineral resources! But the French fixation on food and drink also extends to water. Bottled mineral-rich waters from major springs are widely popular, with different waters having different flavors according to their mineral contents. The waters are either still or sparkling (gaseous), and many of their names—such names

Inadequate fossil fuel reserves have led the country to turn to nuclear power plants to make additional electricity.

Vichy and Perrier—are recognized throughout much of the world. Mineral water is also the resource around which many health spas have been built. They provide therapeutic baths, as well as drinking of the waters. Many of these springs are in the volcanic Massif Central and are naturally heated.

The emperor Charlemagne was part of the Carolingian Dynasty, or ruling family.
He was a Frank, a people originally from Germany.

3

French History to 1830

*France secretes, constantly reshapes and feeds on its own past.
Where it has been is, more than for other nations, the explanation
of where it is going. . . . It has a destiny, an extension of
its epic past. . . . It is addicted to greatness.*
SANCHE DE GRAMONT

A deep sense of the past is very much part of French character. Glorious monuments of that dramatic and creative past are revered treasures, the inheritance of the nation. Because of its respect for the past, France exceeds most other countries in its historic-preservation efforts.

The history of any country, France included, is made up both of important individual events and episodes and long-term changes. Short-term happenings, for example, include the French Revolution of 1789–1799 and the Battle of Waterloo that ended Napoleon's power in 1815. Long-term trends affecting France include broader alterations over extended periods, such as took place during the Renaissance and the Industrial Revolution. In this chapter, you will get a brief glimpse of both of these kinds of history. In providing that glimpse, it will be necessary to vastly simplify a very long and complex past.

CELTIC BEGINNINGS AND ROMAN OCCUPATION

France's cultural heritage extends some 480,000 years back in time. Early Stone Age people inhabited the region, including the "cavemen" who left a record of their existence with marvelous painted caverns such as those of Lascaux. Here, however, our history begins with the Celtic Gauls, peoples conquered by the Romans between 125 and 12 B.C. That conquest was partly under the generalship of Julius Caesar (from 58 to 51 B.C.), and resulted in the deaths of a million Gauls, with a comparable number being enslaved—not to mention Roman casualties.

The Celts spoke languages whose origins probably go back to Central Europe or the Caucasus region. Over time, they came to occupy most of Central and Western Europe outside of Scandinavia. Some 60 independent "tribes," collectively called the Gauls, dwelt in present-day northwestern Italy, France, Belgium, and parts of Germany and Switzerland. They farmed, kept livestock, practiced crafts, and frequently fought. They practiced Druidic religion, which included human sacrifice. The French speak of "our ancestors, the Gauls." In fact, the Arvernian Gaulish chief Vercingetorix, who led a brief uprising against the Roman occupation in 52 B.C., is counted as the first French hero— though he was neither French nor notably heroic (he was defeated at Alésia, in Burgundy, and taken in chains to Rome).

We speak of certain things French as being "Gallic," such as the Gallic cock—the French national symbol, similar to our American eagle. Yet there is very little in French culture other than place names that can be traced to the Gauls. There are, for instance, only about 200 Celtic words in the French language.

It is the Romans—whom most French view as having been foreign occupiers rather than ancestors—not the Gauls, to whom France owes most of its "Frenchness." The Romans were the first to unify the territory that is now France. They introduced good roads as well as their stone architecture. They were responsible for the wide dispersal of vineyards and wine-making. They also brought the Latin language, from which the French tongue ultimately evolved. In addition, Romans introduced sizable cities, forms of government and law, and the Roman system of surveying. Important as well were Roman military architecture, Roman agricultural methods, and the Roman alphabet. Christianity was another of the many cultural legacies of the great Roman Empire.

Rome's impact was strongest in Provence, whose traditional architecture is so like that of parts of Italy that the one place could pass for the other. The lower Rhône region contains some of the world's best-preserved Roman structures. They include the Pont du Gard aqueduct at Remoulins, the theater and triumphal arch at Orange, the arenas at Arles and Nîmes, and the little Maison Carrée temple at Nîmes (which inspired Thomas Jefferson's design for the Virginia state capitol building).

Despite the occasional rebellion, most Gauls favored Roman occupation, even if grudgingly. It was the Romans who established peace—the *pax romana*—among the often-warring Celtic tribes and afforded protection from the German tribes across the Rhine River. Peace and security, along with improved transportation and the presence of Roman legions, led to great enhancement of Gaul's prosperity.

THE "DARK AGES" AND CHARLEMAGNE

During the Roman period, many Germans, especially Franks, were allowed to settle in some numbers in Gaul, where they became increasingly Romanized. During the fifth century, more and more Germans and Scandinavians penetrated into Gaul uninvited, plundered there and, in many cases, settled down and established local kingdoms. Rome, too, fell to barbarians, and the end of the Roman Empire in the West is conventionally set at 476 A.D. After that date, both cities and foreign trade declined in Gaul, as elsewhere.

Franks formed a small minority of the post-Roman population, but they successfully conquered and ruled through military force. The Frank Clovis (reign 481–511) established the Merovingian Dynasty, selected Paris to be his capital, and adopted many Roman values, including Catholicism (ca. 496). Clovis's Church-anointed coronation at Reims in 507 A.D. marks the foundation of France as a nation. From 987 on, most of France's later kings were also crowned at Reims. (Interestingly, even though the Franks were Germans, only 520 German words survive in Modern French.)

The Merovingians under Charles Martel ('Hammer') defeated invading Arabs in 732 A.D., near Poitiers, ending the expansion of Islam in Western Europe. The Carolingian Dynasty, which succeeded the Merovingian, expanded under the great but ruthless leader Charlemagne (742–814) and the Franks came to control most of old Gaul plus additional areas. In 800, Charlemagne was crowned emperor by Pope Stephen II. Following Charlemagne's death in 814, the Frankish kingdom was in 843 formally divided into three parts. Although omitting about one-fifth of today's country, the part known as West Francia became the territorial foundation for the future development of the country we know as France.

THE MIDDLE AGES: ABBEYS, CHURCHES, AND CHIVALRY

During the 800s and 900s, France was plagued by raiders such as Muslim Saracens, Hungarian Magyars, and Norse Vikings sweeping into the territory. The latter finally settled around the mouth of the river Seine in 910, evolving into Normans and adopting the emerging French language.

The Capetian Dynasty, founded in 987 and lasting until 1328, rescued West Francia from a tendency to break into separate fragments. During their rulership, the Capetians crystallized the concept of "France" as an almost personified political and territorial entity—a perception persisting to the present day. Hugh Capet (reign 987–996) was the first French-speaking king.

This period also saw the rising importance of monastic orders, as Catholic monasteries came to control vast lands and wealth. A Benedictine reform movement began in 909 at Cluny in Burgundy. In 1095, the greatest religious architectural complex the world had seen was consecrated there. Another order, the Cistercian, was founded in France in 1048. Religious pilgrimages grew in importance, including across central and southwestern France on the road to Spain's Santiago (Saint James) de Compostela. From 1095 to 1291, knights and other warriors from France were the most important players in five crusades to recapture the Holy Land for Christendom. The crusades fostered a sense of French national identity. The fairly brief presence of Europeans in Palestine led to the importation of much Eastern knowledge into Europe, including ideas important to geography and architecture. Pointed arches, stained-glass windows, and some other features characteristic of Gothic architecture probably have their sources in the East.

In 1137, Eleanor, daughter of William of Aquitaine (a southwestern province), married France's Capetian crown prince, Louis. Later that year, he became King Louis VII. Eleanor's dowry included what today amounts to the southwestern quarter of France. After being divorced 15 years later by Louis, she later married Henry Plantagenet, duke of Normandy and count of Anjou, who in 1154 became king of England. This resulted in her now-reclaimed lands being added to Henry's, which included not only England, but also present-day France's northwestern quarter. Half of France now belonged to England, in the so-called Angevin Empire. The situation was further complicated when the scheming Eleanor abandoned Henry and established her own court back on the continent, in Poitou. The resulting situation, intolerable to France, led to 300 years of political and military conflict, including the "First Hundred Years' War" (1159–1299), in which France, under kings Philip Augustus and Louis VIII, regained all but the province of Guyenne.

Despite its often devastating wars and its crusade against religious heretics in the South, during the Capetian Middle Ages France saw rising prosperity, rapid population growth, an increase in the size and importance of towns (*bourgs*) and their burghers (*les bourgeois*)—that is, manufacturers and merchants—plus professionals of various kinds, and acquisition of Langedoc. This is attributable, in part, to milder weather, improved agricultural technology and methods, reclamation of wild lands for farming, and the proliferation of water mills and windmills for both grain-grinding and manufacturing, plus a general rise in trade. Many new agricultural villages were established, bringing their number close to today's approximately 30,000. Commercial fairs became numerous in the north, and craft, merchant, and professional guilds wielded ever-greater power. A literature in the French language emerged for the first time.

The Capetians, unable to produce a male heir, were succeeded in 1328 by the Valois Dynasty. The glory days of the Capetians were to be followed by troubled times, which included economic slow-down as new reclaimable farmland and military plunder were exhausted and as trade patterns shifted; peasant uprisings occurred (and were viciously suppressed), and there were war and epidemic.

King Edward III of England believed that the reigning French King, Philip VI, held the throne illegitimately. Edward declared himself king of France and invaded. The result was the devastating Hundred Years' War (1345-1453). During the lengthy conflict, the English ultimately were driven from all of France except the Channel port of Calais. Joan of Arc provided one dramatic aspect of the war. The young French peasant girl and religious visionary who had rallied the French forces was captured by the English, who burned her at the stake as a witch (partly because she wore male battle dress).

Medieval towns, like Carcassonne, France, were often surrounded by a high, fortified wall to protect its inhabitants. Traffic in and out of the town could be controlled at the gates in the wall.

During the Hundred Years' War, actual fighting occurred during only about a fifth of the years. The long, if intermittent, conflict saw the first use of gunpowder with cannons (Battle of Crécy, 1346), which revolutionized warfare, contributing to the end of knights in armor and to modification and then abandonment of castle building. At the end of the war, many castles were demolished, fostering the rise of kingly control and the decline of seigniorial fiefdoms—small local areas ruled from castles by individual nobles, who both taxed and defended their people. A French standing army was created for the first time. This greatly increased royal power and set the stage for future monarchical control, a decline in the feudal system, and territorial expansionism.

As if war were not enough, in 1348 the Black Death, or bubonic plague, struck Europe. One-third of France's population died during this and later plagues over the next century.

Working-class individuals who survived the plague's ravages prospered. Labor shortages caused wages and standards of diet to rise. Much empty farmland was available, leading to a portion of the peasantry becoming independent of the nobles.

The European Middle Ages continue to fascinate us. It was a time of opulent excess, violence and cruelty, and vicious exploitation of the people. At the same time, there was piety and religious self-denial, idealistic romantic chivalry, charity, and creativity in the arts. France was at the center of it all.

THE RENAISSANCE AND THE WARS OF RELIGION

In Italy during the 1400s, a rediscovery of and renewed appreciation for classical Greek and Roman knowledge and art began. It was fueled in part by the arrival of Byzantine Greeks fleeing Turkish invaders and in part by contacts with Arabs, who had preserved much Greek and Roman knowledge. The beginning of papermaking and printing with movable type in Germany around 1450 spread to France. A French printing shop opened in Paris in 1470. Relatively inexpensive printed books revolutionized learning and the spread of ideas, now within the grasp of "commoners."

This Renaissance, or 'Rebirth' of classical knowledge, affected France in the late 1400s, slightly later than it did Italy. King Francis I (reign 1515–1547) became enthusiastic about Italy's Renaissance movement and imported it to France. Under the later Valois kings, the population recovered from the plagues, and monarchs continued to centralize power. The feudal system, in which local lords ruled over serfs (farmers tied to their lands) and usually provided little support to the king, declined further. The monarchy became increasingly absolute, and its ties to the church loosened. Display of royal grandeur—large palaces, ornate works of art, pomp and ceremonies, and the like—became ever more elaborate as the kings endeavored to increase their power and prestige.

During the latter half of the 1500s, many Valois kings were

young, sickly, or weak. During this period, from 1560 to 1574 the Italian widow of Henry II, Catherine de' Medici, reigned as regent for her underage son. She was one of the few women of the era to possess strong political and economic power.

The late 1500s brought many problems to Western Europe. The climate became much colder (an episode called the "Little Ice Age") and struggles for power increased. Religious tensions also became intense because of the emergence and spread of Protestantism. This movement, begun by Martin Luther in Germany in 1517, was promoted most effectively in France by John Calvin beginning in midcentury.

French Protestants were termed "Huguenots." Their numbers grew rapidly, threatening the established Catholic Church. The consequence was the savage and devastating Wars of Religion, fought between 1562 and 1598. Henry of Navarre (Henry IV) succeeded to the kingship in 1589 as the first of what became known as the Bourbon Dynasty. Although he had adopted Catholicism in order to secure the throne, he was sympathetic to Protestants. In 1598, his Edict of Nantes granted qualified freedom of worship to Protestants. Meantime, because of almost continuous fighting, both the people and the national economy had suffered severely.

THE SUN KING AND HIS SUCCESSORS

Protestants benefited from the Edict of Nantes for less than 90 years. Henri IV's successor, Louis XIII (reign 1601–1643), showed much less sympathy with Protestants. It was his successor, Louis XIV, however, who was most responsible for returning France to exclusive Catholicism. He was to become France's most powerful and long-reigning king (reign 1643–1715). Because he likened himself to the Greek sun god, Apollo, Louis XIV was referred to as the Sun King. When he assumed the throne in 1643, he came to it as an anti-Protestant. In 1685, Louis revoked the Edict of Nantes, thereby reestablishing Catholicism as the state religion and resuming the persecution of Protestants.

As a consequence, a quarter of a million Huguenots fled to England, the Netherlands, Germany, and even the American South. This was a great material loss to France, since many Huguenots were skilled artisans.

The seventeenth century experienced a Catholic Counter-Reformation. It began as a movement to revitalize Christian religious and moral values, but developed into an effort to out-compete Protestantism. One result was the building of many huge and elaborate churches in the new Baroque style.

During this time, the empire of the Germanic Hapsburg Dynasty was expanding. Already claiming Austria, Spain, and the Netherlands, it was beginning to encircle France. From 1618 to 1648, much of Europe was engulfed in the ravaging Thirty Years' War. France entered the conflict in 1635, and the size of its army increased tenfold. During this period, the centralization of power and an already huge bureaucracy increased. France won against Hapsburg Austria and gained considerable territory, including much of Alsace, Rousillon, Artois, and Picardy. Immediately after the war, however, France suffered the "Fronde" (1648–1652). This was a period of state bankruptcy and civil war against centralization and the power of the church through cardinals who served as principal ministers to the king. Ultimately, Louis assumed the role of principal minister himself, thereby completing the centralization of power and gaining ironhanded one-man rule.

Louis's military engineer, the Marquis de Vauban, fortified France's frontiers. The country engaged in three wars between 1667 and 1713, acquiring in the process Flanders, Franche-Comté, and Strasbourg, but the wars were very costly to the economy. During this period, too, the French lost their holdings in French Canada to Britain.

Louis XIV encouraged a cult of the personality by royal display of dazzling magnificence. As a result, the seventeenth century came to be called *le grand siècle* ("the great century"). Louis also worked to make the French family a microcosm of the state, encouraging male authority and wifely subordination. He also locked away prostitutes and others with whose lifestyle he disagreed. Yet, in this era of excess and repression, French playwrights and other authors, as well as artists and scholars, flourished. Thus, the Scientific Revolution got under way, creating ways of thinking about the world that increasingly competed with those of the Church.

THE FRENCH EMPIRE: BEGINNINGS AND EXPANSION

During the Renaissance, Portugal and then Spain began overseas exploration and conquest. They established huge empires, mainly in the Americas, becoming wealthy and powerful from plunder and mining precious metals. France and England took note and initiated their own quests for empire. France established colonies in Canada, in Louisiana (sold to the United States in 1803), and in the Caribbean. It also gained a foothold in India and established trading stations on the coast of West Africa.

Gaining mineral and luxury manufactured products from these regions was important. So, too, was the commercial production of tropical and subtropical crops. From the colonies came rice and indigo, the dye used to impart a dark blue color to denim (from *de Nîmes*). Denim was used for cowboys' jeans in France's Camargue and later was introduced in America by Lévi Strauss. Sugarcane, however, was the most important colonial crop. African slaves were brought into the Caribbean to produce it. The French port of Nantes was prominent in this tragic commerce in human beings.

Growing international trade boosted the importance of port cities such as Nantes, Bordeaux, Brest, and St-Malo. However, France's imperialism increased its friction with the equally ambitious British, inducing the "Second Hundred Years' War" (the third, really) between the two expanding powers. Although foreign possessions went back and forth between the two countries, France ended up the loser. An especially bitter loss was its near-expulsion from India. These wars severely taxed France's economy; but at least they were largely fought at sea and on foreign soil. Despite the wars, the eighteenth century was one of much-improved roads and increases in trade, food production, and population within France, itself.

THE ENLIGHTENMENT AND THE FRENCH REVOLUTION

Although French glory and culture continued to have a huge international influence, the Sun King's successors, Louis XV and Louis XVI, found it increasingly difficult to maintain absolute power. The times, themselves, were against the kings. Social and economic barriers between the landed nobles and the affluent middle class were blurring, and the number of bourgeois grew rapidly. Expensive wars (including aid to the American Revolution) led to higher taxes and declining state solvency, which sparked popular resentment.

Perhaps most importantly, the printing press allowed wide dissemination of information and ideas. Antiroyalist and anticlerical sentiments flourished. So did the philosophies of the Enlightenment, a literary and scientific movement in which writers like Montesquieu and Voltaire spoke the desirability of a more rational, reasonable, and egalitarian (equal) society. These and other French thinkers of the time also had a major influence on the development of democratic ideas in what was to become the United States. In the face of science, religion was on the decline. The rate of literacy climbed dramatically, and people eagerly discussed ideas, including democratic ones. Popular opinion began to exert an ever-greater pressure on royal politics.

Finally, on July 14, 1789, the situation exploded. An angry Parisian mob stormed the Bastille, a political prison by then little used but still a symbol of the repressive royal regime. The French Revolution had begun. The French Revolution was both a triumph of the philosophy of freedom and equality and a time of destructive excesses and mob tyranny. "It was the best of times, it was the worst of times," as Charles Dickens characterized it, "it was the spring of hope, it was the winter of despair." It certainly ended up changing not only France, but also the world.

Change had actually been going on for some time. The bourgeois-professional class was becoming increasingly important, at the expense of the nobility and clergy. The revolution itself was preceded by population pressure, rising prices, and expensive wars. Following the destruction of the Bastille, rule by the people was established. A Declaration of the Rights of Man appeared, feudalism was abolished, as were the church tithe and sale of public offices. Liberty, equality, and fraternity (brotherhood) were declared, and a red cap that had been the ancient badge of emancipated slaves became a symbol of the revolution. Paris's heraldic red (associated with the republic) and blue (which has Carolingian and Capetian associations) were added to the traditional white of the Bourbons' royal national flag to yield the tricolor, which has remained France's flag to the present day.

The king was not immediately deposed, but was made a constitutional monarch by the new National Assembly. France's traditional provinces, once governed by local nobles, were replaced by a greater number of smaller departments administered by central-government appointees (prefects). High office was opened to all classes, and all property-owning males were accorded the vote. Restrictions on private enterprise in business and other economic activities were lifted. Church-owned real estate—amounting to 6–10% of the cultivatable lands—was confiscated to pay off government debt. Reforms guaranteed freedom of speech and of the press. The metric system was created as well.

Violent opposition soon clouded these promising beginnings. Colonies revolted, as did the conservative Vendée in France's west. Austria and other European powers attacked, fearful of the possible spread of revolution to their countries. At home, extremism was rampant. There were ruthless massacres, followed by executions—including those of King Louis and his queen, Marie Antoinette. The (First) Republic was declared in 1792.

Social radicals known as Jacobins seized power in 1793, enforcing populist reforms by means of the "Reign of Terror." The guillotine was developed to decapitate (behead) political prisoners. Several hundred thousand opponents of the revolution were killed and another 150,000 fled the country. The Reign of Terror saw further centralization of power, the temporary replacement of Catholicism by an invented Cult of the Supreme Being, and brief use of a new calendar. An enormous army also was formed to oppose foreign invasions.

In 1794, the Jacobins were overthrown, but still, things moved from crisis to crisis. Then, in 1799, a military officer from Corsica named Napoléon Buonaparte (later, Bonaparte) engineered a coup d'état to reestablish stability, and had himself declared absolute consul.

THE FIRST EMPIRE AND THE NAPOLEONIC WARS

Napoleon was an absolutist. His rule was totally personal and almost as far from democratic as one could imagine. The press was muzzled, political activity restricted, and women's rights reduced. A royal court—his—and aristocratic titles were reinstated. Napoleon did reestablish political stability. He also approved a system of civil law that came to be called *la Code Napoléon* (the Napoleonic Code, which remains the legal code of Louisiana today).

Napoleon, who in 1804 declared himself emperor, pursued a vigorous program of expansionism on the continent. Soon, as a result of his ambitious conquests, much of Western Europe came under his control. His wars were financed mostly with the spoils of conquest; he depended largely on troops conscripted in the conquered countries. France itself remained peaceful and prosperous until 1810.

Napoleon ultimately found that he had overextended his capacity to conquer and control. Particularly disastrous was his invasion of Russia (1812–1813), in which half a million men were lost. It was British opposition, however, that proved to be

Napoleon Bonaparte was one of the world's most famous, and infamous, leaders. Remnants of his system of civil law persist today. He was also both a war-mongering imperialist and a political stabilizer.

his most difficult obstacle. Napoleon was soundly defeated and deposed in 1814. He made a comeback in 1815, however, but was defeated again in the Battle of Waterloo (in Belgium) and was exiled for good. France's boundaries reverted to those of 1792, and the Bourbons were restored, in the form of backward-looking Louis XVIII.

Napoleon was a military genius. Some historians see him as having been an egotistical, war-mongering monster. Others judge him to have been a disseminator of the values of the revolution who, had he not been defeated by the British, might have created a European or even world federation and avoided future world wars. One thing that is indisputable is that Napoleon lost for France most of her first overseas empire.

The Eiffel Tower was built in about two years and was completed in March 1889 as part of a temporary Universal Exhibition celebrating the French Revolution. Its usefulness as a radio-broadcast antenna allowed it to remain as a permanent structure

CHAPTER

4

France in the Modern Era (1830–Present)

The Frenchman wants to superimpose his personality on the vanquished. . . he thinks he can do nothing in the world more profitable than to give him his ideas, customs, and fashions.

JULES MICHELET

In many respects, a three-day Paris revolution in 1830, which installed Louis Philippe as king, marks the beginning of the modern era for France. In that year, the country began to rebuild an overseas empire, as the conquest of Algeria began. Important political changes occurred as well, including a reduction of lavish living by kings and the endorsement of more civil liberties.

POST-NAPOLEON FRANCE AND A NEW NAPOLEON

During the eighteenth century, the steam engine-powered Industrial Revolution began in Britain. Adopted in France during the nineteenth

51

century, the economic revolution introduced mass manufacturing and railroad building and saw the growth of financial institutions. France rapidly became the world's second-leading industrial power, after Great Britain. French-manufactured products such as silks, gloves, and porcelains became widely recognized abroad and prized for their high quality.

Cities expanded, and a swelling laboring class reacted with socialism to capitalists' exploitative treatment of employees. For various reasons, discontent grew not only among factory workers, but also among the peasants, the ruling class, and the well educated. An economic crisis in 1848 led to another brief revolt in Paris, forcing Louis Philippe to abdicate; a Second Republic, with universal male suffrage, was declared. The new president, Louis Bonaparte—a nephew of Napoleon I—proved not to be a democrat, however, and declared himself President for Life in 1851 and then Emperor Napoleon III the following year. Unfortunately, Napoleon III did not possess many of his famous uncle's talents.

One of the emperor's few real achievements was the physical transformation of Paris into a city whose grandeur reflected Napoleon III's self-image. Broad boulevards and new monuments (such as the Opera) were built, helping create the striking city that we know today. Much of the metropolis was modernized and sanitized. Elite and middle-class residences congregated near the city center. The outskirts were left largely to the workers, forming a "red (socialist) belt." This pattern persists to the present, although today middle-class residence in the outer suburbs has become increasingly common.

The Second Empire saw the takeover of Nice and Savoy (1859), as well as of overseas possessions such as parts of Indochina and of West and equatorial Africa. France also was involved in the construction of the Suez Canal, completed in 1869.

Dark days loomed, however. Germany, formerly a collection of small independent states but now uniting under the Prussians, was becoming an expansive power to be reckoned with and even feared. France's provinces of Alsace and Lorraine were vulnerable, because they were substantially German-speaking. In 1870, battle broke out. The French were roundly defeated. Napoleon III was captured and deposed, Paris was taken, and a harsh peace was imposed in 1871. Germany annexed Alsace and much of Lorraine. This Franco-Prussian War was the first act in the modern military struggle between these two powers, especially over the key iron and coal deposits of the border regions. World Wars I and II were to be the second and third acts.

THE THIRD REPUBLIC: PEACE, PROSPERITY, IMPERIALISM, AND THE GREAT WAR

After the fall of Napoleon III, a Third Republic was declared, which lasted until 1940. Although the political system merely tottered along much of the time, with very frequent changes of government (110 in 70 years), this was an era of great events and great changes.

After the Treaty of Berlin in 1880, in which the European powers agreed to carve up Africa among themselves, France's new empire expanded greatly. Eventually, it grew to include some 3 million square miles (7.7 million square kilometers), making France the world's second-greatest colonial power after the United Kingdom. Commerce went hand in hand with colonization, governance, and attempts to impose French language and culture on the native peoples of the conquered areas.

At home, modernization of farming progressed, leading to increased rural prosperity and better nutrition. Running water, gas, electricity, and telegraph offices became common in cities. Canals, railways, and roads expanded, and in 1900 Paris's Métro (subway) was opened. Factories multiplied in the coal districts of the north (steel, chemicals, and automobiles) and around Lyon (textiles). A symbol of this was erection of Paris's Eiffel Tower (1885–1889), made entirely of steel beams and rivets. Trade unions were legalized in 1884.

During the period 1890 to 1914, prosperity widened, as

did consumerism. Newspapers became widespread, and both literature and art flourished. Social programs slowly progressed. "Naughty" public entertainment, such as the "can-can" dancers at the Moulin Rouge cabaret, also flourished. Some people expressed concern over what they saw as increasing decadence. With railroads to provide transport, wintertime resort towns on the French Riviera boomed.

The Catholic Church vigorously resisted the growing modernism of thought, social relations, politics, and lifestyle. But an increasingly freethinking society made church, the monarchy, and harsh authoritarianism increasingly irrelevant. The institution of public (as opposed to religious) schooling, with instruction in French, further eroded conservative church influence and boosted bourgeois values and a sense of national linguistic, social, and political unity.

The brief period of stability and prosperity came to a brutal end in August 1914, when World War I broke out. France had been angered by its humiliating loss of the Franco-Prussian War and wanted Alsace-Lorraine back. Many people were worried by the rise of socialism, high living, and atheism. A war, some believed, could rekindle a sense of serious national purpose.

In World War I, France, Britain, and Russia (The Triple Alliance) fought the central powers of Germany and Austria-Hungary. The combatants became bogged down in trench warfare. Tanks, poison gas, and limited aerial bombing were used for the first time. Casualties (including from disease) were horrendous; the world had never seen such carnage. The Triple Alliance won—France retrieved Alsace-Lorraine and gained Germany's African colonies of Togo and Cameroon, but the costs were incalculable. France suffered 1,385,000 combatant deaths, 2,850,000 soldiers disabled, and another 450,000 imprisoned or missing. Some 200,000 civilians died as well, not to mention millions of farm animals. Much of northern France was devastated. Almost a million buildings were demolished, half of the country's industry was destroyed, and transport

The soldiers are on the British front lines in France during World War I. Almost an extension of the Franco-Prussian War, the Triple Alliance was victorious over Germany and Austria-Hungary but at a great cost.

lines were badly disrupted. Nearly an entire generation of young men was wiped out or left physically or emotionally handicapped. France had become a nation of widows and spinsters (women who never marry). Enormous quantities of resources had been squandered, and war debts were high; the franc declined and taxes rose. The French received huge war-damage payments from Germany, but the resulting German bitterness worked to France's detriment a few years later.

As the war ended, France was struck by another shock—the Spanish influenza epidemic of 1918–1919 killed some 166,000 people in the country. In order to encourage population recovery, starting in 1920 medals were given to women for having numerous children. During the war, many women had joined the work force, but the lack of younger men nevertheless led to a need to import foreign labor. These practices contributed to social divisiveness and the Communist party split from the Socialists.

The 1920s saw the rise of radio and of labor-saving devices.

Also, in 1929 the Maginot Line—a defense against potential German invasion—was authorized. The effects of the Great Depression were felt during the 1930s, and despite incentives the birthrate dropped. Leftist governments introduced various social reforms, but rearmament began as well. Unfortunately, the 1920s and 1930s proved to be only a brief "time-out" in the Franco-German conflict.

WORLD WAR II

Following World War I, the Treaty of Versailles (1919) had disarmed Germany. Under Adolf Hitler's Fascist Nazi regime in the 1930s, however, Germany began to rearm and then to expand its territory at the expense of its neighbors. Fascist Italy, under Benito Mussolini, soon allied itself with Germany to form the Axis. Militarily unprepared to oppose the Axis, Britain and France signed the Munich Agreement recognizing the German seizures. But in 1939, matters escalated to a war footing. Until 1940, little happened on the battlefield; the German and French armies glared at one another from behind the fortified Siegfried and Maginot defensive lines. But then, German tank units, with air support, struck like lightning.

The Germans made a ten-day run around the end of the Maginot Line, through neutral Belgium. Now nearly encircled, French and British troops escaped only by sealift from the channel port of Dunkerque (Dunkirk), involving thousands of private boats. The Germans reannexed Alsace and Lorraine and occupied northern and Atlantic France. Ten million French refugees fled before them. The puppet Vichy government (named for the southern town of Vichy) was set up to administer the south. But soon, Germany also occupied Vichy France. Jews were persecuted, and many French were removed to Germany to become forced laborers.

These outrages fueled the Resistance (*Maquis*), which although involving no more than 1% of the population, never-theless carried on significant spying and sabotage against the

Local French Resistance fighters greet British troops in their village of Quillebeuf, France, in August, 1944. Such fighters assisted the Allies by spying and carrying out acts of sabotage against the Germans as well as helping downed airmen.

occupiers and helped downed Allied airmen to escape. Many *maquisards* were Communists.

Meanwhile, a former junior war minister who had escaped to England with other French troops began to exert his influence. Charles de Gaulle formed the French Committee of National Liberation and convinced the military in a number of colonies to join this Free French movement. Following the Allies' "D-Day" invasion of Normandy on June 6, 1944, Paris was retaken. It was General de Gaulle who led French troops into the city in triumph.

Allied forces took Germany, and in May 1945 the war ended. The Allies (United Nations) occupied Germany (with the French authorities in the Saar Valley and the Rhineland), and Alsace and Lorraine were returned to France. In the fighting, the Free French had lost 167,000 soldiers. Half a million buildings had been

General Charles de Gaulle (center) celebrates with the people of the city of Bayeux after the Allied liberation of German-occupied France. De Gaulle went on to become the foremost politician of post-war France.

destroyed, including most northern factories. Much of northern France's agricultural breadbasket was a moonscape of bomb and shell craters. And there were bitter reprisals against those who had collaborated with the Germans—around 10,000 traitors were executed and 35,000 were imprisoned.

THE FOURTH REPUBLIC

After the war, the task of reconstruction received crucial help from the United States in the form of aid from the Marshall Plan. Some social progress occurred in France. Women finally received the right to vote (1944), and a social security program was instituted (1945). The conservative de Gaulle, who had ruled from 1944, stepped aside in 1946, and the new Fourth Republic nationalized some key industries. No political party held a majority. Governments came and went (25 in 13 years), with various coalitions among Communists, Socialists, centrists, and rightists. De Gaulle remained on the sidelines; although many feared that he would seize power again in order to stabilize politics, this did not occur.

DECOLONIZATION, THE ALGERIAN WAR, AND THE FIFTH REPUBLIC

World War II had changed much of the world. Colonies began to clamor for their independence and the war-weary great empires were breaking up. Rebellions broke out in Madagascar and French Indochina. In the latter, Communist Vietnamese rebels (Viet Minh) thrashed the French at Dien Bien Phu in 1954. Between 1946 and 1977, France granted independence to most of its former possessions, including those in Indochina, although it did retain several former colonies. Some newly independent former possessions became members of the French Community. Member countries (in an arrangement similar to the British Commonwealth of Nations) maintained some weak links to France and received preferred economic status. France continues to have military pacts with some and to give aid to all.

Postwar decolonization proceeded well enough in most areas, with Indochina being a major exception. France, however, was loath to grant independence to its North African possessions, especially to Algeria (an overseas department), since a million ethnic French resided and owned property there. Many, in fact, had been born there. These *pied noirs* ('black feet,' that is, Europeans with their feet in Africa) considered Algeria to be their home and were fearful of the consequences should an Arab government take over. Nor was France anxious to absorb this large population. In 1954, Arabs of the *Front de Libération Nationale* (FLN) began attacks on the French.

The war in Algeria became increasingly one of terrorism, torture, and other appalling atrocities on both sides. When

France showed signs of negotiating with the FLN, military leaders attempted a coup against the Paris government. Charles de Gaulle was called out of retirement and given emergency authority to deal with the crisis. A new constitution was drafted in 1958, instituting the Fifth Republic, in which the president had much greater powers. There was no practical way to retain Algeria, so de Gaulle wisely granted the country independence in 1962. Many French conservatives, however, believed this to have been a traitorous act. Some dissidents engineered assassination attempts against the president, and the OAS (*Organisation Armée Secrète*) attempted another coup, bringing France close to civil strife. By the end of the Algerian War, some 20,000 French and several hundred thousand Arab Algerians had died. About 800,000 "black feet" did relocate in France, particularly in the South.

FRANCE TO THE PRESENT

In 1949, the North Atlantic Treaty Organization (NATO) was formed to create a deterrent to the growing threat of the Communist bloc—the Soviet Union, People's Republic of China, and the Eastern European Soviet satellites. The "Cold War" and nuclear threats continued to throw a shadow over people's sense of security. France developed its own nuclear-bomb capability (1968) and withdrew its forces from NATO's military command. This withdrawal was part of a French policy that indulged in some political nose-thumbing at the country's allies—particularly the United Kingdom and the United States.

For three decades following World War II, France experienced greater political stability, a rising birthrate and lowered deathrate, and the world's highest economic-growth rate. Economic growth involved state economic planning, protectionism, and close cooperation between government, financial institutions, and businesses (including nationalization of some companies).

An agrarian society was transformed into an industrial one. Tractors greatly increased per-capita production on farms. The resulting decrease in rural labor requirements contributed to massive migration to cities. Plumbing, appliances, and telephones became widely available. A system of superhighways was initiated. Supermarkets began to replace small grocery businesses. Two million laborers were attracted from Portugal and Spain, and another half-million came from North Africa. Leisure activities were encouraged, second-home ownership rose, and five-week vacations were mandated. The dingy gray buildings of smoke-grimed Paris were given a bath, from which they emerged refreshingly "new." Yet, low-rent housing for workers, working conditions, and the quality of education were poor. In May 1968, for these reasons and others (including as a protest against the U.S.-led Vietnam War), Paris exploded. Students and workers began rioting in uprisings that shook the nation. The tense situation was made worse by police overreaction. After the riots, the city covered many of its stone-paved streets with asphalt so future rioters could not pull out paving stones to use as missiles. Some reforms followed, although there was a conservative backlash as well. De Gaulle retired (for a second time) the following year.

In 1951, France and West Germany signed the Coal and Steel Treaty, designed to share the border-country resources that had more than once provoked war. Then, in 1957, the Treaty of Rome created the free-trade Common Market among six Western European countries. Over the following years, membership has expanded, economic rules have become more comprehensive, and the political role has become increasingly prominent. The name changed to the "European Economic Community," then to the "European Community," and is now the "European Union." In 2002, most members adopted a new and shared currency, the euro (€). Primary goals of this partial confederation include eliminating risk of further European wars and creating a body strong enough to compete with economic and political giants such as the United States. and Japan. France has been the dominant member, although recent expansion of membership (to 25 at this writing) has somewhat diluted its influence.

At a meeting in April 2003 in Strasburg, France the European Union's Parliament officially agreed on the inclusion of ten new candidate countries: Cyprus, the Czech Republic, Estonia, Hungary, Latvia, Lithuania, Malta, Poland, Slovakia, and Slovenia.

From the mid-1960s, France's fortunes were generally less positive than during the previous three decades. A declining birthrate had advantages, but it also lowered consumer demand and thus prosperity. Industrial production declined, unemployment rose, and the OPEC-generated petroleum crisis of 1973-1974 hit France hard. The country had little domestic oil, and imported three-quarters of its petroleum. As a result of this crisis, France elected to develop nuclear power, despite its risks.

For some time, the Fifth Republic's governments had been conservative. In 1981, however, the country took a sharp turn to the left. A new Socialist president, François Mitterand (1981–1995), nationalized most major industries, insurance companies, and banks. Fully a quarter of the economy was in government hands. Increased economic regulation, plus greatly expanded and expensive social-services programs, led to monetary inflation, low industrial growth, and soaring unemployment. Soon, even many French Socialists sought to replace leftist ideological decision-making with a more pragmatic approach (including encouragement of private investment in shares of nationalized companies to staunch the outflow of funds).

The 1980s and 1990s saw dramatic rises in automobile and television ownership, but crime also jumped as unemployment soared to 12%. Rising crime, in turn, stimulated a right-wing, anti-immigrant political backlash, especially under the leadership of Jean-Marie Le Pen. Nearly a third of France's people are either immigrants (8%) or descendants of immigrants.

Under Mitterand, Europeanization accelerated and anti-Anglo-Saxon sentiment diminished—although a 1977 law against *franglais* (English words entering the French vocabulary) remains on the books. The Maastricht Treaty of 1992 paved the way for European political and monetary integration. In 1994, the undersea Channel Tunnel ("Chunnel") was built near Calais, to connect the rail systems of Britain and France.

In 1995, a fairly conservative government under President Jacques Chirac, former mayor of Paris, took the presidency back from the Socialists. One trend under Chirac has been further deregulation and continued privatization (begun in 1986) of most companies nationalized under the Socialists. Some changes have been required by the European Union. Yet, a close relationship between state and private industry continues.

Most tourists visiting this country expect to experience the famous French atmosphere of a Parisian cafe, but urban France today is actually a mosaic of ethnicities, languages, and cultural traditions.

5

Population, Culture Regions, and Social Institutions

*Fascinated by progress and not wanting to be left out of the
transformations taking place in the world around them, the French
seem incapable of turning their backs completely on the past.*
JAMES CORBETT

POPULATION

"Fifty million Frenchmen can't be wrong," goes the old saying,
but there are now more than *sixty* million French citizens
in metropolitan and overseas France. They account for
16% of the European Union's population and rank France twentieth
among world countries. Approximately 75% of the country's population is urban, living in towns of 2,000 or more people. This is in a land
traditionally thought of as being rural and agrarian. Since 1950, rural
population has declined drastically as a consequence of agricultural

modernization. Small farmers, especially, suffer from low incomes and declining services in rural areas. Economics have forced many who would prefer to farm into other lines of work away from their land. France's average population density is 279 persons per square mile, but distribution is very uneven.

In 2002, life expectancy in France was an impressive 76 years for males and 83 for females. One of the first countries to achieve low birthrates (in the nineteenth century), France nevertheless experienced a post-World War II baby boom. In the early 1970s, low birthrates were restored. In 2002, France's annual rate of natural population increase was about .4%, much of which was contributed by residents of foreign origin. Immigration adds perhaps another .18% each year. Today, France has more than four million foreign residents.

At the 1999 census, one-third of all households were couples with at least one child, 26.8% were childless couples, and 7.3% were single-parent families, a figure much lower than in America. Households of lone individuals accounted for 30%. Availability of the contraceptive pill, a lowering of the average French couple's ideal family size (2–3 children), and more women working, have led to deferred childbearing and lowered birthrates (fewer than 2 per mother). As a consequence, France also has an aging population that will have to be supported in retirement. Too, an aging work force is a handicap in an era when energy, flexibility, innovativeness, and mobility are asked for.

Average age in 1999 was 37 years, a figure that is rising. The age structure was: under 20 years, 25.7%; 20 to 59, 53.9%; 60 and older, 20.4%. The average age at first marriage was 27 for women and 29 for men.

FRANCE'S CULTURAL REGIONS

Metropolitan France is not a culturally homogeneous country containing only one important ethnicity, the "French." France includes, in fact, several regions in which not only is the traditional ethnicity not French, French is not even the first language of thousands, sometimes hundreds of thousands, of people.

In 1800, one in four "Frenchmen" could not speak any French and another one in four only very badly, and even today a quarter to a third of the country's native population can speak a regional language or dialect. The historically most important regional division in France is between the French-speakers of most of the relatively cool and rainy northern two-thirds of the country, and the people (*les méridioneaux*) of the warmer, drier Mediterranean, Atlantic, and Massif Central south or *Midi* ('Midday'), where the *langue d'oc*, a tongue closer to Latin than is French, formerly held sway (where *oc* is the word for 'yes').

Standard French—one of nine *langue d'oïl* dialects (in which *oïl* means 'yes')—emerged from Latin in the Île de France (greater Paris region) under residual Celtic and later Germanic influence and spread from there as the power of Paris gradually expanded outward. The other *oïl* dialects have been diluted to the point that today most northerly regions possess only regional *patois*—"deformed" versions of standard French (as in Appalachian English).

The *langue d'oc* is actually a web of six dialects in three main divisions, running from Spain to Italy. The name of the traditional province of Languedoc, lying to the west of the lower Rhône River, derives from the general name of the tongue, while the province to the east of the Rhône is known as "Provence" (from the Latin *Provincia Romana*), and the name of its dialect, Provençal, is often used to refer to all the *oc* dialects, as is "Occitan."

In some areas, the *langue d'oc* continues to be spoken among country people, mostly in the home (although everyone is now bilingual in French), but fewer and fewer young people are learning it.

Although France—including today's Midi—is largely fully francophone (French speaking), some of its corners retain significant populations whose first language is neither French nor Occitan but some other tongue, plus even greater numbers of people who have at least some understanding of that tongue. One of these regions is French Catalonia, just over the border from Spain's large Catalan-speaking province of Cataluña (Andorra, the tiny Pyrenean country between France and Spain, is also Catalan speaking). Catalan is closely related to the *langue d'oc*. As in other linguistic-minority regions, Catalan continues to be eroded by French, but the strength of Catalan culture and language in prosperous neighboring Spanish Catalonia buttresses the idiom in France, where Catalan promises to endure more robustly than Occitan in nearby regions.

Like Catalonia, the Basque Country straddles the French-Spanish border, formed by the Pyrenees Mountains, but it faces the Atlantic rather than the Mediterranean. Although the Spanish section is much more populous and industrially developed than the French, the French *Pays Basque* is a quite distinctive region in its own right. The French language continues to supplant Basque, an ancient tongue unrelated to other European languages.

Among traditional Basque mountain life ways, sheepherding is the most prominent; Basque emigrant herders have been important in the sheep-raising industries of certain other parts of the world as well, including in the western United States. The male Basque's sartorial signature is the navy-blue *beret basque*—whose mid-twentieth century working-class popularity all over France has since waned in favor of the cloth cap.

On the Armorican Peninsula is the old province of Brittany, home of Armorican Gauls in Roman times and further settled by other Celts during the fifth and sixth centuries, when many Brittonic-speaking Celts fled from the Saxon and other invasions of England. The Bretons and the Welsh share legends concerning King Arthur. The province was not annexed by France until 1532 and maintained considerable separateness for another two and a half centuries. Like Celtic Ireland, it is a very conservative and religious Catholic region, with many unofficial local saints and a multitude of religious processions called *pardons*.

The stone folk houses of the scattered farmsteads still standing in Brittany today remind one of those of Celtic parts of the British Isles. Like many areas of Celtic regions of the British Isles, too, Brittany and Normandy possess numerous stone walls and hedgerows on farms. Such *bocage* country is strictly a northern phenomenon in France.

Numbers of speakers of the Breton language can still be found in the western parts of the province, although the language is on the decline, with less than a fifth of the population speaking it, mostly as a second language; only about 6% of people under 25 use it regularly. Despite considerable disaffection among Bretons and efforts at cultural revival, there is little separatist effort in contemporary Brittany.

The Romance-Germanic linguistic border does not coincide with the frontiers between countries; it cuts through France's Flanders, Belgium, France's Alsace-Lorraine, and Switzerland.

Contemporary France's Germanic northeastern corner has, over the last couple of hundred years, passed, like a football, back and forth between France and Germany. The old provinces of Lorraine (native land of Charles de Gaulle) and Alsace were largely German-speaking; and although most Alsatians' loyalties lie with France, one of two dialects of German is still the first language of most older Alsatian country folk; 90% of the population can speak Alsatian, although in the province as a whole, French is the first language for 85%. Alsace's older architecture is Germanic in style, and there are many picturesque villages with fairytale-like half-timbered houses whose steep roofs are covered with flat tiles. Although Catholicism is strong, northern Alsace has France's highest concentration of Protestants.

Eastern Belgium, just to the North of France, is French speaking (Walloon), whereas western Belgium (Flanders) is Flemish speaking. Flemish and Dutch are close dialectical cousins. As mentioned above, some of Flanders (*Flandre*) lies on the French side of the frontier, which was fixed in 1713. Not only can Flemish (*flamand*) still be heard spoken there, but the older architecture, mostly in brick, is more akin to that of Belgium and the Netherlands than it is to that of other parts of France

Separated from mainland France and situated out in the Mediterranean Sea, is the large island of Corsica (*Corse*), Napoleon's birthplace. The traditional language and culture are much more akin to those of Italy's Tuscany than to those of France, and historically included the custom of *vendetta*, blood feud between families—personal, family, and clan loyalties being paramount. Of France's "non-French" regions, Corsica has seen the most violence in the course of a struggle for some autonomy.

Metropolitan France also has some important immigrant populations of non-French, including non-European, origin. Today, the European Union (EU) permits free migration among its member countries. Portuguese, Italians, and Spaniards became very numerous even in pre-EU times. Non-ethnically French, non-EU residents derive mainly from former colonies and current overseas departments and territories and include considerable numbers of (mostly black) West Indians, Africans and their descendents from subSaharan countries, and North African Arabs and Berbers from Algeria, Morocco, and Tunisia. There are also rather large numbers of Asians of Vietnamese background. In addition, a certain number of Turks figure in France's labor force. There are wandering gypsies as well.

Racial discrimination is not a major concern in France, and laws against it were passed in 1999 (although not involving affirmative action). However, native French expect immigrants to adopt French ways and values and are disdainful of those who fail to do so; the state offers language and other integrationist programs. One point of conflict is the feast of Aid al-Adha, when Muslims ritually slaughter tens of thousands of sheep.

FAMILY, HOME, AND LOVE

The family is of utmost importance in France. "Everything," wrote historian Fernand Braudel, "starts with the family, and almost everything can be explained by it." In the north, the simple nuclear family holds sway. But in the south, the tradition is of Mediterranean-style "community" families in which a patriarch heads an extended family that includes his sons and their wives and children. In Germanic areas of France, a patriarchal family is traditional, with only one son per generation being allowed to both stay home and to marry.

As a whole, French families tend to be somewhat patriarchal, at least in form, although wives and mothers have always played a strong role. Despite families being child-centered, in the past fathers did not overly involve themselves with care of the children. This has changed a bit in recent decades, especially as more and more women have entered the work force. French personal incomes are lower than in the United States, and the dual-income family is becoming the norm.

The Frenchman and Frenchwoman's home has always been his and her castle, and security and privacy are highly valued. There will be shutters on the windows, always closed at night and often during the day, plus a wall—perhaps topped by shards of glass—or a thick hedge around any garden. Even tiny houses and apartments have entry halls from which the rest of the home is closed off by doors, so that callers may be received there, or at least screened prior to being permitted to enter the rest of the home. In the interior, doors to bathrooms and bedrooms are kept closed even when not in use. It is less common to be invited for a meal at a person's home (as opposed to at a restaurant) in France than in the United States.

French families stress closeness and express affection by means of the classic two- or three-kiss embrace as well as in other ways. French children leave home at a later age than in America. In many respects, the French have been more successful than the Americans in maintaining meaningful family relationships among the generations. Younger people sometimes experience such a high level of togetherness as rigid and stultifying, but in fact it is highly beneficial—socially, educationally, and behaviorally—to almost all concerned.

The value accorded to the family is signaled by the existence of a High Council for Family Affairs and Population. Still, the French family has changed since the early 1970s. Parental authority has been eroded (though less so than in the United States). Divorce rates have risen to about one in three nationwide and to one in two in Paris. This is much lower than in the United States or in other European Union countries.

There are many types of households other than traditional families. About a third involve single persons who are divorced or have never married. Homosexual couples are legally recognized, although not universally accepted.

One seemingly "antifamily" trend is the rise of cohabitation since the late 1960s. One couple in six, of young adults of the opposite sex, is living together without formally marrying. Cohabitation is legally recognized as a state equal to marriage. In reality, these are usually serious relationships (often, trial marriages) and many such couples tend to marry if pregnancy ensues. Others may feel that a nonbinding relationship is more "authentic," and, in fact, one in four children is born out of wedlock.

As of 1999, there has also been a legal arrangement intermediate between cohabitation and marriage, called a "pact." Such arrangements have led to higher rates of sexual fidelity earlier in life. But the incidence of marital infidelity nevertheless remains relatively high in France, despite a heritage of Catholic guilt about such behavior. In France, sex is seen as a private matter left to personal choice. The question here is more one of openness and tolerance than of permissiveness and personal promiscuity.

Love, as distinct from mere sex, has made a comeback, and fear of acquired immune deficiency syndrome (AIDS) has fostered sexual restraint. Whereas in the past, marriages were often largely matters of family alliances, wealth-preservation, and convenience, leading to either resignation or rebellious infidelity, today's young people are far more likely to look for common interests and genuine affection in a marriage, not simply security or social position. We may also observe that the French love household animals: there is more than one pet for every two people. Many rural men keep hunting dogs, and well-behaved lap dogs are even commonly seen in restaurants!

SOCIAL CLASSES

"France is not one society but many societies," wrote historian Fernand Braudel. In addition to having regional differences, France was once a land of enormous contrasts in recognized rank and in wealth. Considerable rigidity existed with regard to mixing among the various socioeconomic classes. Much of French politics since 1789 has had to do with the ongoing tensions between the values of a conservative and hierarchical tradition on the one hand, and the radical and egalitarian one created largely at the time of the French Revolution on the other. The French class system was the one that most stimulated Karl Marx in his development of the theory of class struggle. The socioeconomic classes have their traditional stereotypes:

- The cultivated airs of the upper-class aristocracy, whose inherited titles, though having no legal status today, remain socially significant.

- The adaptability and the social pretensions of the upper middle class.

- The *middle* middle class concern for the bourgeois values of money, comfort, and order.

- The respectable, egalitarian, independent, and frugal lower middle class, comprised of tradespersons and small shopkeepers.

- The naïve, suspicious, cautious, and greedy peasantry.

- The uncouth and radical, mostly urban, working class.

Like most stereotypes, these have some basis in reality, but are largely exaggerations and not universally applicable.

Whereas class and regional distinctions have begun to blur, especially with a shift from blue-collar to white-collar employment and with much labor migration, young people still generally marry within the social, occupational, and regional groups in which they grew up. Class-consciousness remains strong, relating less to affluence than to cultivation of taste and sophistication.

The presence of large numbers of foreign-born inhabitants and their descendants in modern France raises various issues. Single-ethnicity ghettos are discouraged but do exist, and, as mentioned, foreigners are expected to adapt to French ways. Native French find immigrants troubling, especially if they are not assimilating. This is not a matter of race, but of culture: clinging to one's ethnic identity threatens the ideal of a unified national culture.

RELIGION

As of 1999, approximately 82% of the population was classed as Roman Catholic. However, a long history of negative attitudes toward the clergy, especially during the revolution, plus increasing rationalism and secularism, has resulted in a very high rate of nonobservance. Today, some 25% of "Catholics" are nonbelievers. As one author (James Corbett) put it, "The French are Catholic more by tradition than by conviction." Many enter churches only for ceremonies such as baptisms, marriages, and funerals. The pronouncements of Rome on personal matters such as sex, contraception, and abortion are widely dismissed.

Calvinist and Lutheran Protestants comprised a mere 1.64% of the population in 1999. Much of the Protestant community fled following the 1685 revocation of the Edict of Nantes. The Jewish population, reduced during World War II, hovered at 1.29%. Islam, on the other hand, had grown rapidly with immigration from North Africa and stood at

Most French are Roman Catholics, in name at least. Many French Catholics go to church only for special occasions, such as weddings or the baptism of newborns.

6.89%. Too, .68% (mostly Vietnamese immigrants) were Buddhist and .34% Eastern Orthodox Christians (for example, Russians and Greeks).

There always used to be a village priest, but today the Catholic Church is experiencing a shortage of clergy. It has responded with withdrawal of full-time priests from smaller churches, which are served, if at all, only by priests who travel from town to town.

SETTLEMENT AND HOUSING

The hierarchy of settlements from small to large in France is: farmsteads, hamlets, villages, market towns, cities, and metropolises. Paris, whose metropolitan area holds more than 11,000,000 inhabitants, is overwhelmingly the largest of the urban agglomerations. Thirty-eight other cities have 100,000 or more inhabitants. With some 75% of its people living in towns or cities, France is a highly urbanized country.

As the job market becomes more urban, so does the work force. Only a quarter of the population lives in small villages or rural valleys like this one near Megeve, France.

Housing shortages are commonplace, and costs are high, especially in Paris. Rent controls established in 1948 unintentionally discouraged private construction or renovation of rental properties. In response, during the 1960s the state erected many large, dismal social-housing blocks, the most notorious being in the Parisian suburb of Sancerre. Today, these are mostly inhabited by the poor, the unemployed, and the elderly, many being immigrants. Since 1986, rent controls have been phased out and private construction of apartment houses has resumed. Some of the aging public-housing projects began to be renovated and landscaped during the 1990s.

In France today, perhaps 45% of the people live in apartment houses, and 56% of single-family house-dwellers live in homes they own. Second homes are owned by 10% or more, as well. Home ownership is highly valued, just as land ownership was to people's peasant ancestors. It provides security and a sense of having one's own domain.

Unlike in the United States, where wooden houses are the norm, in France older houses are constructed of stone while contemporary ones are of cinder block and concrete or, in some areas, hollow tiles or brick. France has fewer developments containing "cookie-cutter" houses. Architecture is more customized, although it must, by law, conform to the regional style. Good insulation in new homes is encouraged by tax incentives, to conserve energy.

SOCIAL SECURITY: SOCIAL SERVICES, RETIREMENT, AND HEALTH

Most French persons believe in the need for a government-provided "safety net." The resulting costs of the country's many social service and welfare programs is high, but citizens are unwilling to cut them back. The Ministry of National Solidarity is in charge of many of these generous programs, as well as of immigration.

The French healthcare program, under the Ministry of Health, is also generous (although less so than the free national health program in the United Kingdom). It covers from 60 to

100% of costs, and includes maternity and disability insurance, as well as family allowances for dependent children. A non-government committee of workers' organizations and employers negotiates price agreements with representatives of the health-care providers, and basically runs the system. The choice of physicians is up to the patient. Costs of medications, whose prices are set by the government, are also reimbursed.

France ranks third in the world when it comes to per-capita health-care expenditures and, despite an oversupply of physicians, these expenses are increasing as health-care costs escalate. French health care is at the top of the World Health Organization's rankings, and the French hold the record for frequency of utilizing the system and of taking medications. There are both public and private hospitals. Despite being a Catholic country, France also pays for requested birth-control aid, which has been legally available only since 1967 (the country has allowed abortion since 1975).

All kinds of social security, not just that for retirees, are funded largely through direct contributions from employers (representing a third of their wage bills) and, to a lesser degree, employees. However, what is not paid for in this way must be made up from general taxes. The social security system accumulated such large debts that interest rates and the value of the franc were affected, resulting in an overhaul of the system in 1995.

There are unemployment benefits of 60 months' duration. For decades, unemployment has been a problem in France, and currently stands at about 9%. One response has been to decrease the length of the workweek to 35 hours, to increase the length of paid vacations to six weeks, and to lower the (optional) retirement age from 65 to 60. Benefits (and even retirement age) vary according to job category and years of employment.

Life expectancy in France is almost 80 years, as compared to 76 in the United States. Infant mortality is about .6%. Despite the cultural emphasis on food and drink, obesity is surprisingly uncommon—much less prevalent than in Germany or the United States. Death due to cardiovascular problems is lower than the European average. Wine is thought to offer some protection. Still, cardiovascular disease is the principal causes of death, followed by cancer and automobile accidents. Cigarette smoking is more common in France than in the United States, but has declined somewhat in recent years. Cigarette advertising has been banned since 1993. Nonetheless, annually there are approximately 60,000 deaths attributable to tobacco use.

Although the country is a transfer point for the shipping of illicit South American cocaine, Southeast Asian heroin, and European synthetic drugs, illegal drug use in France, while serious, is lower than in the United States. This consumption is largely of "soft" drugs, but hard-drug use is growing, especially in slums. Interestingly, the French have the highest level of consumption of legal tranquilizers in the world.

EDUCATION

The French prize education, which they recognize as being an important pathway to both polish and position. Education is compulsory from ages 6 to 16, and literacy approaches 100%. Most schools are public and administered by the Ministry of Education and Research. There are also state-subsidized Catholic schools, which are particularly popular in Brittany. The basic curricula of all schools, whether public or Catholic, are identical, although some flexibility has been accorded to the regions. Catholic schools account for 15% of primary pupils and 20% of secondary students. Many parents select private schools not for religious reasons, but because there is more discipline and more after-class supervision. Most French teachers are civil servants. The school year is shorter than in the United States, but school days and weeks are substantially longer. Standards are high.

Many young children go to preschools for two- to five-year-olds and kindergartens for those aged five and six. All children

Education in France is considered more rigorous than in the United States and the nation's literacy rate of 99 percent is evidence of this.

attend primary school (equivalent to U.S. grades one through five), middle or junior high school (grades six through nine), and academic, vocational, or technical high school (grades ten through twelve). The type of high school (lycée) one attends is determined on the basis of examinations taken at the end of ninth grade. Even academic students, though, must have some vocational training. At age 17, one takes the corresponding baccalaureate examination, success in which symbolizes graduation and is prerequisite to higher education. Although the academic exam has eight specialized varieties (math-physics carries the most career clout), it is comprehensive and grueling, being taken over a period of three weeks. About 78% of those who take the exam pass it these days, far more than in earlier times.

There are 86 public and 4 Catholic universities. Fees are low, and half the students pay nothing, but the institutions are correspondingly underfunded and provide less than pleasant study environments. One may earn any of various degrees, including a *licence* (more or less a Bachelor's degree), and a *maîtrise* or a *diplôme* (roughly, Master's degrees). A few scholars write a substantial thesis and gain the coveted *doctorat* (approximately, a Ph.D.). Students are evaluated less by individual class tests than by very lengthy subject-matter examinations at the end of the course of study. France has some 71,200 primary schools, middle schools, and high schools and employs nearly 850,000 teachers. About 10% of students enrolled in higher education are foreign.

Education was shaken to its roots during the events of May 1968 when university students, particularly in Paris, revolted against their mode of education. The type of education offered was very structured, stressed upper-class values and nationalism, and involved much rote learning. Students rebelled against both this kind of instruction and the inaccessibility of their teachers. In the years since, education has seen a shift from the classical to more experiential learning and creative activity. Yet, much rote learning remains and too much originality continues to be stifled. There were more student demonstrations in 1986.

France's traditions are especially humanist, and educational choices at the universities once reflected this. But today, interest in specializing in literature or philosophy has waned in favor of mathematics and science, which are considered more critical in the contemporary high-tech world. Interestingly, despite a long-established adulation of writers, the French as a whole are not great readers.

The president of the National Assembly, Jean-Louis Debre, passes an honor guard on his way to a joint session of the two legislative houses, the National Assembly and the Senate, at the Chateau of Versailles.

6

France's Government

How can you govern a country with 246 different varieties of cheese?
— CHARLES DE GAULLE

NATIONAL GOVERNMENT

The constitution of today's Fifth Republic—"a subtle blend of authoritarianism and parliamentary democracy" (wrote James Corbett)—provides for a president and for a bicameral legislature consisting of a Senate and a National Assembly.

The president of the republic (currently, Jacques Chirac) is elected for a seven-year term by direct universal suffrage on the part of those over 18 years of age. If no candidate receives a majority, a run-off election is held between the two top vote-getting contenders. There is no vice president. The president appoints a premier (currently, Jean-Pierre Raffarin), who recommends the other members of the cabinet to be appointed by the president; the cabinet is housed in the Hôtel Matignon next to the president's Elysée Palace to the north of the Champs Élysée.

As in the United States, the president is the state's executive officer via his or her policy-setting cabinet of senior ministers, and is commander of the armed forces. In a time of crisis, he or she may assume emergency powers. The president may initiate legislation, but to become law such proposals must be passed by the legislature. Of the total number of bills that the latter considers legitimate, 90% originate with the cabinet, rather than from members of the legislature; the latter mainly amends, accepts, or rejects such bills. If it rejects, the government can still issue decrees to the same effect, or put the bill to a vote of confidence in which case it becomes law unless an absolute majority of the legislature votes censure within 24 hours. The president can also call a voter referendum on a bill. Thus, the president and his government hold unusual legislative power and he or she can also dissolve the legislature and call for elections. However, the deputies of the legislature can oust the government, too, providing something of a check on presidential power.

The *Assemblée Nationale*, which meets in the Bourbon Palace across the Seine from the Place de la Concorde, is composed of 577 deputies, from the same number of electoral districts; in the case of a lack of a majority in a district election, a run-off is held. Terms are 5 years, but, as mentioned, the president may dissolve the assembly at any time and call for new elections, which must take place between 20 to 40 days after dissolution. The 300-plus senators, who are chosen by an electoral college, serve 9-year terms. The *Sénat* meets in the Left-Bank Luxembourg Palace, where members deliberate bills. Although it can be obstructionist in delaying implementation of legislation, the senate's power is limited since if the government so requests, the assembly can approve laws without the senate's concurrence.

France is famous for the size, complexity, inflexibility, and expense of its bureaucracy. It is the state's civil servants, though, who have always kept France operating when crises of government have occurred. These same civil servants have also, not infrequently, tied up government functioning by striking.

REGIONAL AND LOCAL GOVERNMENT

France is not a particularly large country, and political authority is centralized. Unlike in the United States, the political subdivisions do not legislate, but only implement the national laws. In 1972, however, 22 administrative "program regions" were created in metropolitan France (and 4 overseas) to somewhat disperse decision-making. These were reorganized and given greater powers in 1982. Elected regional councils consist of local deputies, senators, and delegates with six-year terms. The councils coordinate regional economic development and professional training and adapt national planning to local conditions.

Each region is made up of a number of departments, of which there are 96 in total plus 4 overseas. At the time of the revolution, departments were established to replace the aristocrat-run traditional provinces of the old regime. Although departments are divided into *arrondissements* (wards), *cantons* (districts), and *communes* (municipalities or townships), it is the commune that is the basic unit of local government. The large number of communes (36,394) makes for serious cost inefficiencies. Communal councils are directly elected; the councils appoint the mayors, who also serve as the representatives of the central government. The Paris-appointed *commissaires de la république* (replacing former departmental prefects) ensure council conformity with national regulations and are in charge of police and security. Departments administer social assistance and local transport and maintain departmental roads and junior high schools. Communes handle urban development and property, birth, death, and marriage records, and maintain local roads and preschools and elementary schools.

POLITICAL PARTIES

Politics are an absorbing interest for the citizens of France. The French system allows for many political parties—a reflection of French individualism. Usually no one party holds the legislature's majority and a coalition government must be stitched together. Philosophical boundaries between parties have become increasingly difficult to detect. In recent decades, the most prominent groups have been Chirac's neo-Gaullist conservative party, the Rally for the Republic (RPR); the centrist collection of parties, the Union for French Democracy (UDF, founded by Valery Giscard d'Estaing); and the Union of the Left, formed by the Socialist party (PS), led by Lionel Jospin, and the French Communist party (PFC), whose power has vastly waned. On the far right, but increasingly influential, is le Pen's National Front (FN); there are several FN mayors in the south. Gradually, the environmentalist parties—the Green party, the Ecology Generation, and the Independent Ecologist Movement—have made some small headway, not easy in an environmentally complacent land.

POLICE AND JUDICIAL SYSTEM

Armed police, wearing their billed pillbox caps, are visible in France. In the cities, it is the police in the strict sense, under the Ministry of the Interior. In the countryside, it is the *gendarmes*, under the Ministry of Defense. In addition, there is the National Security Police (CRS) that responds to demonstrations and strikes, not to mention to terrorist attacks.

France has both civil courts and criminal courts. The former try cases involving disputes between parties, while the latter deal with legal offenses of minor and moderate nature, such as infractions and misdemeanors. Very serious crimes (felonies) are tried in assize courts, which are called into session only when required, and consist of judges from the appeals courts. The rate of violent crime is low, but burglary and robbery are widespread. France abolished the death penalty in 1981. There are also commercial courts and administrative courts. Cases that have passed through the court of appeals without resolution regarding points of law may then be heard by the supreme court in Paris. For consideration of the constitutionality of proposed (not existing) laws, there is the constitutional council; but cases can be brought only by the president, the premier, the president of either legislative house, or 60 deputies, and not by private individuals or entities. Unlike in the United Kingdom and the United States, France's judicial proceedings are heard only by judges; there are no juries. Also, judicial precedent is not considered; each case is judged without reference to past decisions. The president's minister of justice, or high chancellor, appoints judges, so even the judiciary is not independent of the executive branch.

THE EUROPEAN UNION

As mentioned above, the European Union (EU) is an expanding consortium of European countries that is moving deliberately in the direction of common policies at the continent-wide level. Among these is, in addition to free trade, the goal of universal public-sector balanced budgets. Many EU countries, including France, have adopted the shared euro (€) as a replacement for their individual national currencies.

France has had a tendency to either dominate EU policy setting, or bend the rules when its interests are at stake. In particular, France has dragged its feet in relinquishing trade protections and government subsidies of agriculture and certain industries. France has been able to get away with this behavior because, as geographer Thomas M. Poulsen put it, "In many ways France is the pivotal state of Western Europe. . . the largest and most powerful country. . . ."

DEFENSE

Before 2002, when the draft was eliminated, young French males were subject to ten months of national service: military, defense, or technical aid to overseas departments and territories, or international cooperatives. The 275,000-person French armed forces include an army, a navy, and an air force, overseen by the minister of defense. The famous French Foreign Legion, comprised of non-French nationals under French officers, is part of the army. During de Gaulle's presidency, France developed nuclear-bomb capability and missile delivery systems and distanced France militarily from the North Atlantic Treaty Organization; however, France has since had a partial reestablishment of cordial relations with NATO.

France is the world's fourth-largest exporter of arms, which sometimes creates political controversy.

France's wide variety of climates allows the cultivation of a wide variety of food crops, including grapes in this vineyard near the village of Cramant. The country's food supply is therefore more self-sufficient than in most European nations.

7

France's Economy and Communications

France is one of the most richly endowed countries of Europe.
— *Worldmark Encyclopedia of the Nations*

France ranks fourth among countries in terms of its economy, with a gross domestic product (GDP) of around $1.5 trillion. Per-capita purchasing power is the equivalent of about U.S. $24,500 per year (compared with the U.S.'s $34,100 in 2002).

AGRICULTURE

France is an agriculturally favored country—60% of its land is arable and over half is cultivated—and produces prodigious quantities of food. It is the only country in Europe to be self-sufficient in basic food supply (although importing tropical products such as cotton, tobacco, and vegetable oils). Further, France is one of the continent's leading food exporters (especially of wheat, beet sugar, wine, and beef).

Yet despite its importance, agriculture employs only about 2.6% of the labor force, reflecting a sharp decline since 1970—by as much as half in the case of small farmers—and contributes less than 3% to the gross national product (although food-processing is an important industry). France resists bigness, and its food-processing plants tend to be too small to be efficient in the world marketplace. Therefore, most of the country's food exports are unprocessed or only partially processed.

France's agriculture has been somewhat slow to modernize, and farmers have frequently demonstrated against quotas and low crop prices resulting from surplus production and foreign competition. They long depended heavily on various subsidies, many of which have been recently reduced or eliminated under the EU's Common Agricultural Policy, or CAP, which aims to eliminate surpluses and supports.

One problem that has affected French agricultural efficiency is that of farm fragmentation. Traditionally, peasant farmers wanted to have a variety of types of land in order to raise a variety of kinds of crops and animals for subsistence. This desire generated individual family holdings in the form of multiple scattered parcels, rather than a pattern of large single blocks of farmland as is usual in the United States. Then, after primogeniture (inheritance by the eldest son only) was abolished in 1804, inheritance among the several offspring led to breaking up of the already multiple parcels into ever more numerous and ever smaller ones. Eventually, an original small number of modest-sized plots became hundreds of tiny, scattered plots. All this made for decreasingly viable and efficient farms, especially for contemporary commercial, mechanized, and chemically managed farming of one crop as opposed to subsistence farming of a variety of products. In recent times, there have been efforts to consolidate fragmented parcels into fewer, larger ones, or to establish overall management of extensive areas in which owner-ship remains fragmented. Under this consolidated management, individual land parcels can be bought and sold as investments in the larger operation, like shares of stock. There are some 680,000 farms in France, many of which are small; although half of the farmers and their spouses also hold other jobs, they form a much larger percentage of the working population than in the United States. Average farm size today is about 100 acres—half again as large as a decade earlier, but still not terribly efficient.

Contemporary agriculture, with its heavy use of fertilizers and pesticides, is productive, but has taken an environmental toll. Principal crops are wheat (for famous French bread, croissants, pastry, and pasta), barley, oats, maize (corn), sorghum (as animal feed), sugar beets (for sugar and alcohol; France is the world's second-largest grower), flax (for linen and linseed oil), rapeseed (for oil), potatoes, and wine grapes. France is the world's fifth-largest producer of grain and of meat, and its sales comprise one-quarter of those of the European Community's CAP countries. Market gardens are prominent in the major river valleys near cities.

Livestock is of prime importance, largely for meat, milk (France is the world's fifth-largest producer), and hide production. There are 20 million cattle, 16 million swine, 9.8 million sheep, a million goats, and many horses (horseflesh is eaten, though declining in popularity); poultry and rabbits also play significant roles. Dairy products such as cheeses (nearly 300 varieties), yogurt, and butter figure importantly in French cuisine, as do eggs, but milk is drunk only by children.

Although underdeveloped, the seafood industry is also notable, and includes not only the taking of wild fishes, crustaceans, and shellfish, but also much aquaculture on the Atlantic coast (oysters, mussels).

MANUFACTURING

France's mineral resources and mining and its electrical-power industries were described in Chapter 2. Construction and civil engineering are also highly important, and France's Bouygues is one of the largest construction companies in the world.

Manufacturing is a major part of the French economy despite a relative lack of high-quality ores and other raw materials within its borders. The Peugot auto factory in Mulhouse is only one in a country that ranks third in car production.

In manufacturing, France ranks fourth among the world's countries, after the United States, Japan, and Germany, and this activity accounts for about a quarter of the GDP. Slightly over one-quarter of the labor force is employed in manufacturing, which is very diverse. Owing to major destruction during World War II, France built modern plants afterward, but these are aging today. Geographically, factories are concentrated around Paris, in northern France's old coal basin, in Alsace and Lorraine (where there is still iron ore and coal), and around Lyon and Clermont-Ferrand. The French preference is for middle-scale, innovative, and high-quality manufacturing, rather than mass production.

Although still important, the French steel industry suffered much during the economic crisis of the 1970s and has declined owing to cheaper foreign sources and to substitution by aluminum and plastics.

Machinery is a leading product of French factories. France remains the third-largest producer of automobiles, although foreign competition has been eroding its market share. Michelin is the world's leading manufacturer of tires. France ranks fourth in chemical manufacture. The country is a leading producer of sophisticated aircraft as well, such as Mirage fighter planes and various commercial aircraft, such as the Airbus, built by Matra-Aérospatiale. France also produces and exports Exocet missiles and other military equipment. Additional leading industries include pharmaceuticals (fourth-largest producer), perfumes, cosmetics, electronics (including telecommunications and information technology), textiles, and food processing. Saint Gobain is the globe's leading glass producer, and Bic supplies the large majority of the world's ballpoint pens, cigarette lighters, and razors.

France's industries have been comparatively tardy in becoming involved in domestic and international mergers to expand companies' reach.

INTERNATIONAL TRADE

Despite widespread suspicion of globalization, several French corporations, including those manufacturing automobiles, are important on the international scene. One may mention AXA insurance, the Carrefour grocery-store chain, and the Thalès defense and electronics industries. France is the world's fourth-largest exporter of goods and the second-largest exporter of both services and agriculture (first in Europe in the latter). The country usually has a trade surplus. Leading French exports include capital goods (machinery, heavy electrical equipment, commercial ground-transport equipment, aircraft), consumer goods (cars, textiles, leather), and unfinished products such as chemicals, iron, and steel. Notable specific exports include nuclear technology and subway systems. In turn, France imports fossil fuels and ores, metals, machinery and equipment of various kinds, chemicals, and a variety of consumer goods and foodstuffs. Nearly two-thirds of France's foreign trade is with other EU countries.

SALES AND SERVICE INDUSTRIES

In France, over 70% of the working population is employed in the service sector. Some 35% of the work force is employed in government and related services; some 17% is involved in the wholesale and retail trades and hotels; approximately 11% is involved in providing real estate and financial services; and 7.4% is engaged in other areas.

Service industries include banking (France is third in the world), insurance (world's fourth largest), securities (seventh largest), and the like. Government work includes taxation, administration, education, public research, transportation, social services, and medicine and public health. Businesses associated with entertainment include the media, sports, and tourism (e.g., hotels and restaurants).

Retail Stores

France has always been known for its small shops: the grocer's, the butcher's, the bakery, the boutique, the dry-goods shop, the tobacconist's, the little hardware store, and so forth. These still exist in large numbers, but since 1957, the spread of supermarket chains such as Auchan, Casino, and Intermarché has badly eroded the small-business landscape, and today huge, inexpensive chain emporiums such as Carrefour, Prisunic, Monoprix, BUT, Mamouth, and several others, are extending the damage.

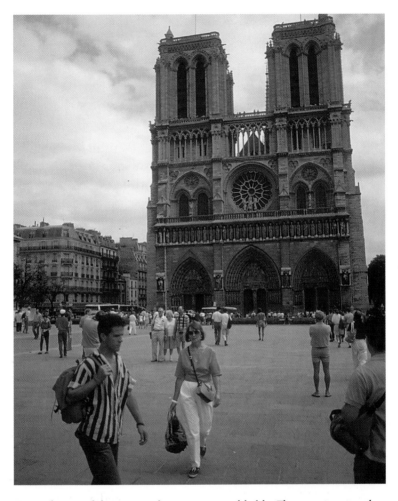

France is one of the top tourism venues worldwide. The country spends a good deal promoting tourism and restoring those monuments, such as the Cathedral of Notre Dame in Paris, that draw the crowds.

Tourism and Leisure

With 70 million foreign travelers a year, France is the world's top tourist destination, with Paris being a particular magnet. Tourism expenditures are a major part of the French economy, especially in less agriculturally or industrially favored regions. The bulk of foreign tourists are from other European countries, but visitors do come from the world over. There is much internal tourism as well. France is the home of the global vacation-village chain, Club Méditéranée.

SPORTS

The French enjoy watching and participating in sports, and physical education in the school system has been improving in recent times. French people tend to prefer sports of skill to those of brute force. In terms of membership in sporting federations, the favorites, in order, are: soccer, tennis, skiing, judo, basketball, rugby, gymnastics, horseback riding, and golf. Interestingly, most of these sports are of foreign derivation. On a less formal basis, there are thousands of lawn-bowling players in every region, especially in the warmer, drier south.

French folks enjoy sports spectacles—the drama, the atmosphere—and play with typical French flair. In fact, in contrast to Anglo-Saxons, in team sports French athletes tend to play more as individuals than as coordinated teams.

The national spectacle of the *Tour de France* bicycle race catches the imagination of almost every French man and woman. Its itinerary circles the country and celebrates France's rich diversity. An American, Lance Armstrong, has won several consecutive recent Tours.

ASSOCIATIONS

Although individualists, the French are social creatures and tend to be joiners: there are some 800,000 associations in the country and nearly half the population belongs to at least one. These groups support specific sports, cultural interests, hobbies, social fellowship, self-help, causes, and so forth.

COMMUNICATIONS AND MASS MEDIA

France has long had an efficient postal service, which comprises part of the PT (*Postes et Telecommunications*) established in 1889. Telephone service was archaic for a modern country until the 1960s; but now, France Télécom (although debt-ridden) is as sophisticated as any such organization in the world. Most businesses and households now have phones. Public phones are activated by "smart" *télécartes*, rather than by coins. Cell phones are everywhere. Also widespread is the *minitel*, a home or office videotext terminal that allows, for a fee, visual display of current information and entertainment of various kinds, as well as the free telephone directory. Home computers, e-mail, and surfing the Net are becoming increasingly popular, although less so than in the United States.

Television is also almost universal, although cable is not well developed. As in the United States, many criticize television for having damaged social life—but just about everyone watches it. While reducing the isolation of rural life, radio, television, and films have also had the effect of eroding regional languages and dialects—despite instruction in Alsatian, Occitan, and Breton in regional schools since 1980. Television news has also contributed to the decline of newspaper circulation, especially of the traditional Paris-based national newspapers such as *Le Monde* and *Le Figaro*. Regional newspapers have declined less, partly because of being aimed at a mass audience and partly because of their detailed sports coverage.

Radio and television stations and channels were once the monopoly of the state (comparable to the BBC in the United Kingdom) and had relatively elevated content. Since the 1970s, many private ones, tending toward the less intellectual material, have been allowed to come into existence. The popularity of American shows such as *Dallas* and *Dynasty* a couple of decades ago has been replaced by a much greater quantity of, and interest in, (government-subsidized) home-grown fare, both in television and the cinema.

Paris is the center of book publishing and magazines, as well as home to the National Archives and National Library, with 13 million books. The country's universities have large libraries as well, and there are many hundreds of local public libraries. France is also a leading player in computer-software development and data-processing.

TRANSPORTATION

In premodern times, France's roads were poor and overland transportation—by coach, wagon, animal-back, and on foot—was slow and uncomfortable. Long ago, France put its rivers to use for boat and barge traffic, and built canals connecting the major streams. The country now has the densest network of navigable waterways in non-Russian Europe. Where available, water transport was far faster, easier, and cheaper than land transport. Today, there are some 9,300 miles (14,966 kilometers) of navigable waterways, of which 4,330 miles (6,968 kilometers) are heavily used. With a couple of hundred merchant ships, France is also moderately prominent in marine transport. French ships carry about half of the country's imports and exports. France's shipbuilding industry is technologically very advanced.

After Great Britain, France was one of the first countries to develop a railway system; and though somewhat reduced in mileage since its heyday in the mid-twentieth century, the nearly 20,000-mile (32,186-kilometer) system is still vital to the transport of freight all over metropolitan France. The railway network has been state-controlled since 1937. In contrast to the situation in the United States, passenger rail traffic is still quite important, a situation given a boost by the development since 1981 of the world's fastest train, the TGV, which averages 155 mph (249 kph), cruises at 190 mph (305 kph), and is capable of 320 mph (514 kph). The TGV is much more economical than flying and links Paris, Bordeaux, Lyon, Marseille, Montpellier, and Strasbourg with each other and with Brussels, Amsterdam, Lausanne, Bern, Cologne, and London. The 31-mile (50-kilometer) Calais-to-Folkstone Channel Tunnel ("Chunnel"), completed in 1993 by the British-French consortium Eurotunnel, links France and

A super-fast TGV train races past the Cruas nuclear power plant. For France, nuclear energy has meant freedom from oil producers and nuclear armaments have meant protection from international hostilities.

England. The rapidity of travel from all corners of France has reinforced the focus on Paris. The Paris Métro is only one of several subway systems in France's larger cities.

France's roads and highways are also very extensive—well over half a million miles (804,650 kilometers) paved, some 21,000 (33,795 kilometers) of those being national highways. France possesses the world's densest high-quality road network. Some 6,150 miles (9,900 kilometers) of turnpikes now link major cities. Traffic is heavy, and speed limits are ignored. The automobile accident rate is horrendous, much of which is contributed to by drunk driving.

There is bus service throughout the country, although the French still prefer their private autos. The days of large numbers of people getting around by bicycle, moped, or motorbike are over. Car ownership has come to be almost universal outside of the densest urban areas, with Renault (which now owns Nissan), Peugeot, and Citroën being the major car manufacturers.

France has 268 airports with paved runways. Air France is the state-controlled international airline, and there are two major private airlines. In addition to ordinary jet aircraft, Air France helped pioneer the supersonic (and super-expensive) transatlantic Concorde. The plane, built with British partnership in 1976, was retired from scheduled service in late 2003.

Paris remains the transportation hub, and even today much travel between distant parts of the country must pass through the capital, even when the latter is far off of the crow-flight route.

LABOR

Nearly half the population of France is employed, although unemployment stands at about 9%. The country has a minimum wage. Over half the work force is white-collar, and 30% is employed by the state.

Although they have declined, labor unions figure fairly prominently in France, although only about 8% of the labor force is unionized (under open-shop rules). France has the lowest EU union membership rate, which is concentrated among public companies and the civil service. Strikes—usually brief, but often crippling—occasionally occur, including road blockages by truckers and train operators. Many strikes, however, are not union organized; rather, they are coordinated via the *minitel*.

As late as 1965, married women could not take a job or open a bank account without permission from their husbands. As of 1985, though, they have had full equality in the family. Gender-related job discrimination was outlawed in 1972, but persists against women (and sometimes men) in a number of areas of work. Still, women are now very prominent in education, health, and law—but not politics. Many women hold part-time posts.

Unemployment is highest among the youngest and the least skilled. The state maintains (re)training programs for first-time job seekers and the unemployed.

FINANCES AND TAXES

France was a pioneer in finance. The country has the full range of banks, insurance companies, and the like, as well as a lively stock exchange. The bank Crédit Agricole is the world's fourth largest.

Owing to high government expenses—public spending accounts for 56% of the GDP—French taxes are rather high (44% of the GDP). There are both modest progressive individual and corporate income taxes, which yield about 20% of tax revenue but which, traditionally, French citizens have endeavored to evade to the extent possible, as they have evaded taxes on large fortunes. Then, there is the newer, harder-to-evade value-added tax (TVA), which usually exceeds 20% and which applies to nearly all sales and services, at both the wholesale and the retail levels (compare to U.S. state sales taxes of from 5 to 8%, on retail goods only). Some do evade the TVA on labor by hiring workers who are paid off the books. There is also a capital-gains tax—again, widely evaded in part—not to mention local real estate, property, habitation, and business taxes. Both national and local taxes are collected and disbursed by the national treasury. Overall, the French pay a much higher percentage of their income in taxes than do Americans, but they also gain many more services. Since the 1970s, efforts to even out discrepancies in wealth among the regions via subsidies have fluctuated.

Inheritances are much more rigidly prescribed in France than in the United States. Children are favored and estate taxes are high, but especially so for those who are bequeathed a legacy, but are not in the direct family line.

In 1999, France's GDP growth rate was 2.9% per year, and there was a large trade surplus; the inflation rate was approximately 1.3%. It's interesting to note that 10% of the wealthiest families possess 54% of gross assets.

This Carnival float representing the "King of the Third Millennium" leads to the question, "How will France fare during the next 1000 years?" If history is any guide, the country will continue to provide technology, political guidance, and sustenance to the world, yet with a creative and independent spirit.

8

France's Future

The real story of France today is the fight between the old, the pleasant and the accepted and the new modern world which France has entered with one half of the country rejoicing and the other half lamenting the death of the traditional France that had settled all questions long ago.

—D. W. BROGAN

Prediction is always a chancy thing. We may ask, "What will France become in the future, how may she change?" We can give few firm answers, though. What we *can* do is to try to project a short distance into the future some of the trends of recent times, and to at least raise some possibilities with respect to certain matters.

Politically, the Fifth Republic appears to be stable and enduring. Despite early fears of too much presidential power, and despite continuing tensions between the professional, entrepreneurial, and working classes, the republic has managed to proceed relatively successfully through four-and-a-half decades, under both conservative and liberal presidents and legislatures. Still, we may well see efforts to limit presidential prerogatives and to create more checks and balances.

France will remain solidly a member of the traditional Western political bloc, although always wishing to assert its individuality even if that involves being perceived as balky. France seems now fully committed to some form of a united Europe, as long as that Europe functions well pragmatically and at the same time encourages the maintenance of individual national identities—the last long a pre-occupation of the French. In fact, in some ways the European Union is seen as a means of protection of that identity against the force of the American economy and culture. In this context, the large numbers of foreign born and their offspring residing in the country will continue to be a source of friction and controversy, testing France's theoretical commitment to *liberté*, *égalité*, and *fraternité*.

Although France's natural resources are varied, its scarcity of petroleum and natural gas will remain a concern. The need for energy resources will certainly play a strong role affecting its international relations, both with the Arab world and with its traditional Western allies in Europe and North America. Nuclear power will continue to supply a great portion of the country's electrical-energy demand, irrespective of environmental and safety objections on the part of Greens, Ecologists, and some Socialists. A trend from heavy industry toward more high-tech industry, such as telecommunications, high-definition televisions, software, and data-processing, seems likely to continue. Further development and use of cutting-edge transport, such as high-speed TGV trains and successors to the Concorde supersonic aircraft, seem likely.

France's economic difficulties, particularly with respect to unemployment and the agricultural sector, pose major problems that are difficult to solve. France will continue to look for ways to become more competitive globally, but its relatively high labor costs, modest-sized factories, and low agricultural efficiency are impediments. The heavy economic burden of the country's social-services programs poses a major difficulty. Yet few French seem prepared to dilute the state-provided safety net in health care, family services, unemployment benefits, retirement pensions, and so forth. No ready answer presents itself, and unemployment leads to discouragement and unrest. Still, the economy should remain vigorous in many ways, although the country faces some serious environmental challenges. The notion of protecting, as opposed to managing and using, nature has not really caught on in France, although European Union regulations will force some improvements. Globalization will be another challenge, and France has begun to acquire a less provincial and more international outlook, as the country itself becomes increasingly multicultural. Adjustment to economic internationalism will not occur without protests and strikes.

The Paris Basin and, to some extent, industrial Lorraine and international Alsace seem destined to draw ever more ahead of economically less favored central and southern France, despite decentralization efforts and considerable "sun-belt" growth in younger job seekers, North African immigrants, and retirees. Labor migration will continue to be largely from south to north, and Paris's expansion will advance. Still, cities like Lyon, Grenoble, Bordeaux, Toulouse, Montpelier, and Nice, will increase their already growing importance in industry, commerce, and population.

Low birthrates will no doubt continue to characterize the country, which will result in an ever-aging population and greater strains on the social security system. Yet, low or no demographic growth is favorable to environmental protection and lessens some burdensome costs, such as those associated with education. More women are likely to be seen in the work force, and continuing expansion of women's rights and roles seems certain. Yet, the leisure ethic will continue to make inroads on the work ethic.

It is safe to assume that French men and women will long be global leaders in aesthetic areas of endeavor. Strengths include fashion and the decorative arts. The French fascination with the subtleties of human relationships will not soon cease, and certainly the preoccupation with fine cuisine and wines, along with many other attractive aspects of their culture, will persist. As philosopher Paul Valéry put it, "We walk backwards into the future." In short, the French will remain French, although in modified, modernized form.

Facts at a Glance

Official name	French Republic (*République Française*)
Surface area	211,208 square miles (546,996 square kilometers)
Capital (and largest) city	Paris (Paris-region population ca. 11,000,000)
Climate	Temperate midlatitude moist, with Mediterranean subtropical conditions (including summer drought) in the south
Terrain	Primarily plains in the north and west, rugged mountainous terrain in south (Pyrenees), east (Alps), and south central area (Massif Central)
Elevation extremes	Lowest point: portions of Rhone delta, 6 feet below sea level (-2 meters)
	Highest point: Mont Blanc, 15,771 feet (4,807 meters)
Population	circa 61,000,000, of which 1.7 million are overseas; 75% urban; 279 per square mile
Life expectancy	(2002) 77.9 years; males, 75.2 years; females, 83.1 years
Natural increase rate	.3% per year
Literacy rate	99%
Form of government	republic (presidential system)
Legislature	bicameral (National Assembly, Senate)
Head of state	president of the republic
Subdivisions	22 administrative regions, 96 departments, 36,394 communes
Overseas departments	French Guiana (Guyane Française), Guadeloupe, Martinique, Réunion
Monetary unit	euro (formerly, French franc)
Principle agricultural products	grains, sugar beets, grapes and wine, other fruits, potatoes, vegetables; livestock
Important manufacturing industries	steel, chemicals, textiles, perfumes, aircraft, machinery, electronics

Other important industries	tourism, timber, fishing, mining
Gross domestic product	(1999): ca. $1.373 trillion
Official language	French
Religions	Roman Catholic (82%), Islam (7%), Calvinist and Lutheran Protestantism (1.7%) Judaism (1%); the majority of French are nonobservant.
National anthem	*La Marseillaise*
National flag	blue, white, and red tricolor of three vertical bands
National holiday (*fête nationale*)	July 14 (*le quatorze juillet*; Bastille Day)
Most famous monument	Eiffel Tower (*La Tour Eiffel*)
Embassy in the United States	4101 Reservoir Rd., NW, Washington, D.C. 20007; (202) 944-6000
Website	*http://www.info-france-us.org*

125–12 B.C.	Roman conquest of Gaul (Caesar's campaigns, 58–52 B.C.).
52 B.C.	Gaulish uprising, under Vercingetorix of the Arvernii, crushed at Alésia by Julius Caesar.
Second–Fourth c. A.D.	Introduction of Christianity, starting at Lyon.
ca. 250–500	Invasions of Gaul by various German tribes, especially by the Salian Franks under Clovis I ending with Roman withdrawal and establishment of a Frankish kingdom corresponding roughly to Gaul, under Merovingian Dynasty (named for the legendary king-diety Merowech or Merovius).
476	Roman Empire in the West falls, barbarians take over.
496	Merovingian King Clovis I (Louis, reign 481–511) converts to Catholicism, crowned king of the Franks, at Reims; makes Paris his capital.
507	Clovis I crowned king of the Franks, at Reims; marks the founding of France as a nation.
732	Pepin II's illegitimate son Charles Martel defeats Arabs at Tours near Poitiers, ending Islamic expansion in Western Europe
751	Usurpation of Merovingian power by palace mayors Pepin II and III completed, and Carolingian Dynasty founded. Carolingians raid surrounding countries for booty.
800	Charlemagne, king of the Franks (reign 768–814) and Lombards, crowned emperor by the Pope. Carolingian empire includes not only former Gaul but also large parts of surrounding countries.
843	Frankish empire split in three by Treaty of Verdun; one part is West Francia, core of future France, under Charles the Bald.
Ninth and Tenth c.	Saracen and Magyar raids; Norse Viking raiders take, and settle along, lower Seine; in 911, Rollo the Viking establishes duchy of Normandy.
987	Hugh Capet nominated king of France (Île de France), founding the Capetian Dynasty, which lasted until 1328.
1000	Year of the millennium; when Judgment Day fails to arrive, many Romanesque churches built in gratitude.
1066	William, Duke of Normandy, conquers England.
1095	First Crusade announced by Louis IX, at Clermont-Ferrand.

1154	Marriage of Eleanor of Aquitaine to Henry Plantagenet of England; half of future France becomes English territory.
1159–1299	"First Hundred Years' War," English driven from all but Guyenne.
1095–1291	Era of the five crusades to the Holy Land and the Albigensian Crusade against the Cathar heretics around Albi; Languedoc annexed (begun 1209).
1309–1417	Popes reside at Avignon.
1328	Capetian Dynasty replaced by Valois Dynasty.
1345–1453	Hundred Years' War between France and England. England takes much territory but is finally expelled. Battles of Crécy (1346; first use of cannons), Poitiers (1356), Agincourt (1415), and Castillon (1453); Joan of Arc helps lift siege of Orléans, is captured and burned by English (1431). Black Death (1348–1352) and recurrences of bubonic plague in 1360–1362, 1374, and 1382; one-third of population dies.
Fourteenth and Fifteenth c.	Major territorial acquisitions: Dauphiné (1349), Provence (1481), Burgundy (1482). Burgundy (1482).
1470	France's first printing shop established in Paris. Books and learning begin to spread widely, ultimately revolutionizing the control and distribution of knowledge and thought.
1515	King Francis I accedes to the French throne, conquers northern Italy; Italian Renaissance influence on France.
1539	French replaces Latin for legal documents and proceeedings.
1541	John Calvin publishes *Institutes of the Christian Religion*; in latter sixteenth century, his preaching gains many converts to Protestantism.
1560–1574	King Henry II's widow Catherine de' Medici rules as regent.
1562–1598	Wars of Religion; toward end, new (1589) Bourbon King Henry IV issues Edict of Nantes (1598), granting limited freedom of worship.
1610	Publication of René Descartes' influencial *Discourse on Method*.
1618–1648	Thirty Years' War; France enters in 1635, gains much of Alsace, Rousillon, Artois, and Picardy; army assumes great importance.
1643–1715	Reign of Louis XIV, the "Sun King"; France acquires Flanders, Franche-Comté, and Strasbourg. Period of Catholic Counter-Reformation.

1648–1652	Fronde (state bankruptcy and civil war).
1665–1666	Great Plague.
1685	Louis XIV revokes Edict of Nantes, reestablishes Catholicism as state religion. Protestants begin again to be persecuted; 200,000–250,000 Huguenots flee France.
1688	Commencement of the "Second Hundred Years' War" with Britain (to 1815).
1713	French Canada loses to Britain.
1768	Acquisition of Corsica.
1776	Acquisition of Lorraine.
1789–1799	French Revolution; attacks by Austrians and Germans beaten off, Marseillaise becomes battle hymn (1792); monarchy abolished, First Republic proclaimed (1792); Louis XVI executed (1793); Napoleon declared consul (1799).
1803	Louisiana Territory sold to United States.
1804–1815	First Empire: Napoleon I consecrated as emperor (1804); Napoleonic Code of law approved (1804). Napoleonic wars (attempted "liberation" and conquest of Europe); Napoleon defeated at Waterloo by Great Britain and allies and deported (1815); most overseas possessions lost. The Bourbon Louis XVIII given the throne (1815).
1830	Three-day revolution replaces Charles X with Louis Philippe. Conquest of Algeria begins.
1848	Brief revolt deposes Louis Philippe; Second Republic declared, with Louis Bonaparte (Napoleon's nephew) made president.
1851	Louis Bonaparte declares self president for life.
1852–1870	Second Empire: Coup makes President Bonaparte Emperor Napoleon III; Savoy and Nice annexed; Empire ends during the Franco-Prussian War (1870–71) with the French defeated and Napoleon captured; Paris taken, harsh peace imposed; Alsace-Lorraine lost.
1871–1946	Third Republic: Trade unions legalized (1884); secular public schooling instituted (1881), Church disestablished (1905).
1876	*Phylloxera* epidemic begins devastating vineyards.
1894–1899	Antisemetic Dreyfuss Affair divides nation.

1918	World War I, followed by Treaty of Versailles (1919). Millions die.
1918–1919	Spanish influenza pandemic, high deathrate.
World War II	France falls to Germans, Vichy government rules Midi (1942–1944), de Gaulle establishes the Free French (1940); allied invasion of Normandy (1944); de Gaulle in office (1944–1946); women given the vote (1944); social security (1945).
1946–1958	Fourth Republic: Aide under the Marshall Plan, NATO formed (1949); Treaty of Paris (1951) forms European Coal and Steel Community, Treaty of Rome (1957) forms European (Economic) Community (Common Market); nationalizations, social security (1946), women's right to vote (1944); decolonization proceeds.
1954	French defeat by Viet Minh at Dien Bien Phu, Vietnam.
1954–1962	Algerian War; attempted coup against President de Gaulle (1958); Algerian independence in 1962.
1958–present	Fifth Republic: universal suffrage (1962), equal opportunities for women (1972), full family rights for women (1985); decolonization continues through 1977.
1968	Nuclear capability is attained, *'force de frappe'*; in May: student and workers' uprising cripples Gaullist regime.
1969	De Gaulle retires definitively.
1981–1995	Socialist President François Mitterand in office.
1992	Maastricht Treaty calling for EEC integration (European Community).
1995	Conservative Jacques Chirac replaces Mitterand as president.

Glossary

Anglo-Saxons: the English speakers, notably the British and the Americans

aquaculture: fish- and seafood-farming, e.g., oysters, mussels, trout

autonomy: independence, self-governance

Baroque: an exuberant and elaborate Roman-derived architectural style of the latter seventeenth century and the eighteenth century (see Classical)

bocage: landscape involving stone walls, hedgerows, and lines of trees to enclose fields and pastures

bureaucrat: a government functionary (*fonctionaire*), i.e, employee

Celtic: referring to a group of languages that include Erse in Ireland, Gaelic in Scotland, Welsh in Wales, and, in France, Breton; also referring to speakers of Celtic languages and their descendents

Classical: ancient Greek or Roman; by extension, art and architectural styles (especially of the seventeenth and eighteenth centuries) echoing canons of classical antiquity, including of stasis and symmetry; more restrained than Baroque (q.v.)

conservatism: a rightist political and social philosophy emphasizing individual and corporate freedom from state interference but within a framework of strict law and order; resistance to change, adherence to tradition, including religious; often hierarchical

coup de'état: overthrow of the exisiting government

cyclonic storm: a large, rotating weather system yielding precipitation as a consequence of frontal activity

department (*département*): a political subdivision roughly equivalent to an American county

empire: a political entity in which one nation rules one or more other nations

fault line: a break in the earth's crust, along which movement has occurred

francophone: French-speaking

Gaul: the region, corresponding roughly to modern France and Belgium, once inhabited by Gaulish Celtic-speakers (*gaulois*) and conquered by the Romans

Gothic: an architectural style of the twelfth through fifteenth centuries; characterized by combining light masonry walls, large pointed-arch windows with tracery, rose windows, pointed rib vaulting, and flying buttresses

langue d'oïl: the medieval Latin-derived language of northern France, in which 'yes' was *oïl*; the direct ancestor of Modern French

langue d'oc: the Latin-derived language of the southern part of France, especially the old province of Languedoc, in which 'yes' was *oc*; see Occitan and Provençal

leftist: see Socialist

market garden: a farm for the raising of vegetables and/or fruits for nearby cities

massif: a mountain mass or highland

Metropolitan France: France exclusive of its overseas departments (i.e., mainland France plus Corsica)

Méridional/Méridionaux: relating to the South (*Midi*); a person/people of the South

Midi: the southern part of France, characterized by a Mediterranean climate and an Occitan linguistic heritage

nation state: a country based on a nationality, most often defined on the basis of a shared national language

National Assembly (*Assemblée Nationale*; **formerly Chamber of Deputies/***Chambre de Députés***)**: one of the two houses of the French legislature (see Senate)

nationalization: the taking over, by the state, of an industry

Occitan or Occitanian: the *langue d'oc* of the old province of Languedoc; sometimes, *langues d'oc* in general

patois: a nonstandard dialect of a language

pieds noirs: ethnically French persons from North Africa

privatization: returning to private ownership companies that had been nationalized

Provençal: relating to Provence; or, the *langue d'oc* as a whole or specifically the dialect spoken in the traditional province of Provence (from the Latin *Provincia Romana*)

province: a traditional major subdivision of the country, in the past normally ruled by a duke or a count

puppet government: a government of natives controlled by a foreign power

Renaissance: a revival of Greek and Roman knowledge and styles, originating in fifteenth-century Italy and affecting France mainly in the sixteenth century; the style of the period

rightist: see conservative

Romanesque: an architectural style flourishing during the eleventh and twelfth centuries; characterized by thick walls, relatively small, round-arched windows, and barrel vaults

Senate (*Sénat***)**: one of the two houses of the legislature (see National Assembly)

Socialism: a leftist political philosophy favoring ownership of the means of production by the state, with all sharing in the wealth (includes Communism); supports social-welfare programs

Further Reading

Aplin, Richard, *A Dictionary of Contemporary France.* Chicago: Fitzroy Dearborn Publishers, 1999.

Ardagh, John, *Cultural Atlas of France.* New York: Facts on File, 1991.

Ardagh, John, *France in the New Century: Portrait of a Changing Society.* New York: Penguin Books, 2000.

Braudel, Fernand, *The Identity of France 1, History and Environment,* tr. Siân Reynolds. New York: Harper & Row, 1988.

Cartographic Division, *Historical France: Evolution of a Nation* [map]. Washington: National Geographic Society, 1989.

Central Intelligence Agency, *The World Factbook 2001.* Washington: Central Intelligence Agency, 2001.

Chamberlain, Samuel, *Bouquet de France: An Epicurean Tour of the French Provinces.* New York: Gourmet Distributing Corporation, 1957.

Charleton, D.G., ed., *France: A Companion to French Studies.* New York: Pitman Publishing Corporation, 1972.

Corbett, James, *Through French Windows: An Introduction to France in the Nineties.* Ann Arbor: University of Michigan Press, 1994.

de Gramont, Sache and Ted Morgan, *France: Portrait of a People.* New York: G.P. Putnam's Sons, 1969.

de Planhol, Xavier, with Paul Claval, *An Historical Geography of France.* Cambridge Studies in Historical Geography 21. Cambridge: Cambridge University Press, 1994.

Evans, E. Estyn, *France: A Geographical Introduction.* London: Chatto and Windus, 1970.

Fernández-Armesto, Felipe, ed., *The Peoples of Europe.* London: Times Books, 1994.

Henderson, Andrea Kovacs, ed., *Worldmark Encyclopedia of the Nations 5, Europe.* Detroit: Gale Research, 1998.

Jones, Colin, *The Cambridge Illustrated History of France.* New York: Cambridge University Press, 1994.

Michelin Green Guides (*Guides de Tourisme*) [region-by-region tourist guidebooks to points of interest]. Clermont-Ferrand: Manufacture Française des Pneumatiques Michelin.

Noriel, Gérard, *The French Melting Pot: Immigration, Citizenship, and National Identity*, tr. Geoffroy de Lafoucade. Minneapolis: University of Minnesota Press, 1996.

Northcutt, Wayne, *The Regions of France*. Westport, CT: Greenwood Press, 1996.

Pinchemel, Philippe, *France: A Geographical, Social and Economic Survey*, tr. Dorothy Elkins and T.H. Elkins. Cambridge: Cambridge University Press, 1987.

Reed-Danahay, Deborah, France. In *Countries and Their Cultures 2, Denmark to Kyrgyzstan*, ed. Martin Ember and Carol R. Ember, pp. 791–806. New York: Macmillan Reference USA, 1991.

The Economist, Survey: France—A Divided Self? *The Economist, 365(8299): special 20-pp. section, 2002.*

Index

Index

118

Index

Index

Index

About the Author

STEPHEN C. JETT is Professor Emeritus of Geography and of Textiles and Clothing, University of California, Davis. He holds an A.B. in geology from Princeton University and a Ph.D. in geography from Johns Hopkins University. He is a cultural geographer and author of the award-winning books *Navajo Wildlands* and *Navajo Architecture*, as well as of *House of Three Turkeys: Anasazi Redoubt* and *Navajo Placenames and Trails of the Canyon de Chelly System, Arizona*. Jett edits *Pre-Columbiana: A Journal of Long-Distance Contacts*, and his book tentatively titled *Ancient Ocean Crossings: The Case for Voyages to America before Columbus*, is in press.

After college, Jett participated in the Experiment in International Living to France's Versailles and became fluent in French; he has owned rental properties in Provence since 1969 and spends part of each year there. He and fellow geographer **LISA ROBERTS JETT**, who assisted on this book, reside in Abingdon, Virginia.

CHARLES F. ("FRITZ") GRITZNER is Distinguished Professor of Geography at South Dakota State University in Brookings. He is now in his fifth decade of college teaching and research. During his career, he has taught more than 60 different courses, spanning the fields of physical, cultural, and regional geography. In addition to his teaching, he enjoys writing, working with teachers, and sharing his love for geography with students. As consulting editor for the MODERN WORLD NATIONS series, he has a wonderful opportunity to combine each of these "hobbies." Fritz has served as both president and executive director of the National Council for Geographic Education and has received the Council's highest honor, the George J. Miller Award for Distinguished Service.